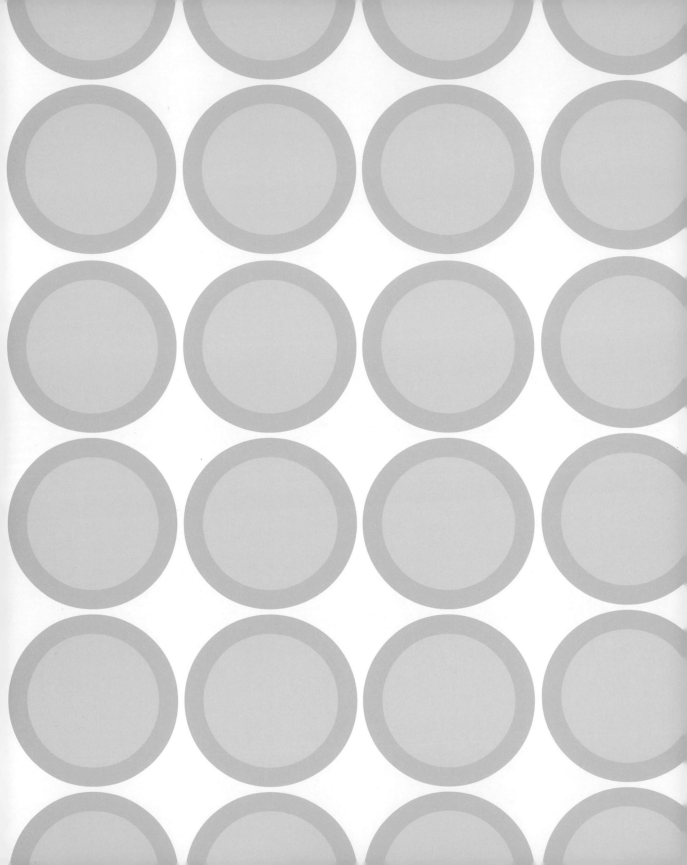

THE CIAO BELLA BOOK OF GELATO & SORBETTO

THE CIAO BELLA BOOK OF GELATO & SORBETTO

BOLD, FRESH FLAVORS TO MAKE AT HOME

F. W. PEARCE & DANILO ZECCHIN

RECIPE DEVELOPMENT & TESTING
BY LEDA SCHEINTAUB

PHOTOGRAPHS BY IAIN BAGWELL

CLARKSON POTTER/PUBLISHERS
NEW YORK

Published in the United States by Clarkson Potter/Publishers, an
imprint of the Crown Publishing Group, a division of Random
House, Inc., New York.
www.crownpublishing.com
www.clarksonpotter.com

CLARKSON POTTER is a trademark and POTTER with
colophon is a registered trademark of Random House, Inc.

Library of Congress Cataloging-in-Publication Data

Pearce, F. W. (Frederick W.), 1962–
  The Ciao Bella book of gelato and sorbetto/
  F. W. Pearce and Danilo Zecchin. — 1st ed.
      p.   cm.
  Includes index.
  1. Ice cream, ices, etc.   2. Ciao Bella Co.
    I. Zecchin, Danilo.   II. Title.

  TX795.P39 2010
  641.8'63—dc22   2009024181

ISBN 978-0-307-46498-9

Printed in Hong Kong

Design by Jennifer K. Beal Davis

10 9 8 7 6 5 4 3

First Edition

page 2: caramel gelato, page 53
this page: madagascar bourbon vanilla gelato, page 26
page 8: hazelnut gelato, page 39
page 11: mexican coffee gelato, page 103

TO THE PASSIONATE FANS OF
CIAO BELLA, WHOSE LOYAL
SUPPORT OVER THE PAST
TWENTY YEARS HAS MADE
THIS BOOK POSSIBLE

CONTENTS

A BRIEF INTRODUCTION TO
GELATO

Italians have been enjoying gelato and sorbetto for hundreds of years. Yet the history of frozen desserts goes back to the Bible, when Isaac offered Abraham goat's milk mixed with snow and told him, "Eat and drink: the sun is torrid and you can cool down." Some say the Chinese invented ice cream: Around 2000 B.C. they were eating a soft rice and milk mixture that was packed in the snow. In ancient Rome, around A.D. 62, Emperor Nero reportedly ate such huge quantities of a snow and ice mixture sweetened with honey that he suffered from "indigestion of snow."

Frozen desserts fell out of favor as the Roman empire declined, but they started to appear in the East. One of Muhammad's disciples invented a way of freezing fruit juices by putting them in containers that were then set in buckets of crushed ice, a system that remained the standard for centuries. The Arabs reintroduced frozen desserts to Italy via Sicily, from whence they spread to Naples, Florence, Milan, Venice, and then all over Europe.

Sorbetto was introduced to the court of the Medicis when a chicken farmer named Giuseppe Ruggieri won a cooking contest with his sorbetto recipe. In the mid-1500s Catherine de' Medici took Ruggieri and his sorbetto to France, where they were received with great success. Soon after, an architect by the name of Bernardo Buontalenti was said to have invented gelato, made with zabaione (see page 58) and fruit and churned over ice and salt. It quickly became part of the social fabric of Italy.

The tradition of gelato making has been passed on from generation to generation, and the flavors available today reflect those recipes. Almost every neighborhood gelateria offers a selection of the classic Italian flavors—including vanilla, chocolate, strawberry, zabaione, hazelnut, pistachio, coffee, stracciatella, and bacio gelato, along with lemon, raspberry, mango, strawberry, and blood orange sorbetti—though the recipes are all slightly different. Each uses regional ingredients or preferred flavoring pastes based on availability and tradition.

> "For Italians eating is akin to religion, and love for food is the only thing that really unifies all of Italy."
> —CHEF DANILO

Gelato eventually made its way to France and England. It was a dessert enjoyed only by the wealthy because of the required preparation time and the amount of ice that was needed. Ice cream came to the United States in the late eighteenth century, and here, too, it was served to the upper classes: It could be found on the menus of state dinners for notable figures such as George Washington and Thomas Jefferson. In the old days, transporting ice cream was impractical and expensive, as it entailed loading a horse-drawn cart with ice and ice cream that the vendor would sell until the supply ran out or melted. It wasn't until the early twentieth century and the invention of mechanical refrigeration and the freezer truck that national distribution was possible and ice cream became widely available for the common folk.

In the past ten years or so, gelato has finally caught on in the United States. Gelaterie have been opening across the country, and gelato and sorbetto are

What Exactly Are Gelato and Sorbetto?

Gelato comes from the Italian verb *gelare,* which means "to freeze," and gelato is a frozen dessert similar to ice cream but made with less fat (or cream) and less air. The extra fat in ice cream can mask its flavors, so gelato tends to be much more flavorful, smoother, denser, and more intense than ice cream. Ciao Bella gelato contains 20 percent air by volume (compared to 50 percent in some American ice cream brands) and 12 percent butterfat (versus 16 to 20 percent in typical superpremium ice cream brands).

Sorbetto is mostly fruit—Ciao Bella's fruit sorbetti contain about 80 percent fruit—along with sugar, water, and sometimes alcohol and flavorings. Sorbetto usually has no cream and therefore little or no fat, so there's nothing standing between you and the flavor, and the taste is incredibly true to the ingredients.

increasingly appearing on restaurant menus. As Americans are becoming more and more discerning about what they eat, they are discovering the flavor and health virtues of gelato and sorbetto: Gelato contains less fat and less air than ice cream, which allows the flavor of its ingredients to come through, and sorbetto is packed with fruit, making it a refreshing, fantastically flavorful frozen treat that's also rich in vitamins and antioxidants. But you don't need to appreciate the health benefits of gelato and sorbetto to enjoy Italy's great gift to ice cream lovers. Anyone can enjoy the taste, the smooth texture, and the incredible sense of refreshment these desserts bring.

THE CIAO BELLA STORY

For more than twenty-five years Americans have been enjoying Ciao Bella frozen desserts. To many, gelato and sorbetto are synonymous with Ciao Bella, with its signature bright, colorful packaging. The company started small and has grown over the years; it now sells about five million pints a year, in all fifty states. The gelato is also sold to about five thousand restaurants, and about 750 flavors have been created . . . so far. But the commitment to making the best-quality gelato continues to be Ciao Bella's guiding principle. Here's a little of the history.

In 1989 I graduated with a master's degree from Cornell University's School of Hotel Administration with the idea of opening a restaurant. Soon after, I realized that that was the last thing I wanted to do. One day I was scanning the *New York Times* classifieds and saw an ad: "Small gelato manufacturing company for sale." I had my eureka moment and knew this was a once-in-a-lifetime opportunity—to combine my business background and my love of food—that I had to grab. Borrowing the necessary funds from my mother, I set out to buy this small business, and small it was: 300 square feet with one ice cream freezer and one full-time employee (me). I had a pickup truck that was insulated with Styrofoam, and I did everything, from developing and mixing the flavors, to driving the truck, to delivering samples to restaurants for chefs to taste.

Our customers included some of New York City's finest independent white-tablecloth restaurants, including Charlie Palmer's River Café, the "21"

Club, and Hatsuhana. Chefs were attracted to Ciao Bella's high-quality ingredients and cutting-edge flavors.

Over the next several years, Ciao Bella moved from its tiny storefront in SoHo to a larger space in Little Italy, and eventually to a 38,000-square-foot operation in New Jersey. In 1994, Charlie Apt joined me as my partner to focus on new business development and growth. The result: a doubling in sales his first year on board and continued expansion every year.

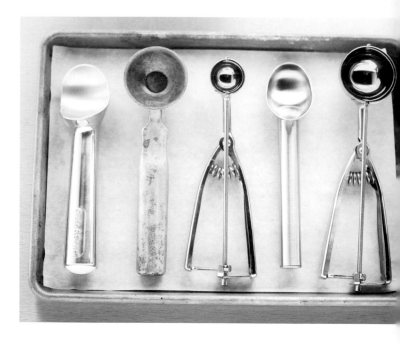

In 1998 Danilo Zecchin joined us as executive chef. Chef Danilo comes from Torino, Italy, a region known for its love of food. He sources the world over for the finest ingredients, such as superpremium Valrhona chocolate from France, Alphonso mangos from India, and raspberries from Oregon, to name a few.

One of Ciao Bella's founding missions was to combine the best of classic Italian gelato with the creativity of modern America. Ciao Bella's goal is to give customers a unique sensory experience—and now with this book you can bring that experience home. We're excited to share the recipes that have made Ciao Bella what it is today and hope that you will try making both your Ciao Bella favorites and flavors you've never even heard of. We also hope that you'll be inspired to create your own signature gelato and sorbetto flavors. Drop us a line at www.ciaobellagelato.com and let us know what you've dreamed up. —FW

MAKING GELATO AT HOME

While these days securing a pint of high-quality gelato may be as easy as walking to your local grocery store, the satisfaction of making your own frozen desserts is something that just can't be measured. Two of the best reasons to go homemade are freshness and choice. Nothing compares with the soft, creamy richness of just-churned gelato. You can truly eat locally by making gelato right in your own kitchen, with the best regional ingredients you can find—including farm-fresh milk and eggs bought at your local farmers' market if you have one nearby. Your gelato can reflect the seasons—strawberry gelato in the spring with vibrantly red just-picked berries, pumpkin and spice gelato as Thanksgiving approaches, and pomegranate champagne sorbetto to bring in the New Year. Making your own gelato puts you in control of the process, and the flavor pairings are limitless. We wish you great success in creating your own personal gelato experience with your favorite fruits, flavorings, and other ingredients.

Gelato making at home and in commercial production share a common trait: both involve two distinct phases. The first phase—making the base or custard—is a very precise process that requires strictly adhering to formulas. In our base recipes, paying close attention to heating time and temperatures and ingredient quantities will pay off in a consistent successful base. The second phase of gelato making is flavoring and freezing. Here is where recipes are less important than personal preference and you get to have some fun in the kitchen.

Fresh gelato is at its best the day it's made, straight from the machine

Although all of our gelato recipes start with the same ingredients included in either of our two bases, in a few cases you will need additional ingredients in the custard-making process or you may need to alter the quantities of the ingredients used. In these cases we have restated the complete recipe for clarity. Examples include Madagascar Bourbon Vanilla Gelato on page 26 and Butter Pecan Gelato on page 76.

if you like it soft, or after firming up for a few hours in the freezer. Anything that isn't eaten on the spot will keep for up to a week in the freezer.

TWO RECIPES, MANY FLAVORS

An ice cream maker might take up some real estate in your kitchen, but the good news is that the time commitment for making gelato is surprisingly short. Active prep time is no more than twenty minutes, and there are only a few ingredients for each recipe. Once you master a simple technique—making a custard base—you will be able to create the dozens of gelati in this book, as well as limitless other flavors, just as Ciao Bella has done. Two recipes—Plain Base (page 22) and Chocolate Base (page 25)—introduce the gelato section and serve as the foundations for all of our gelato flavors. The bases yield about 3½ cups, which is enough to make approximately one quart, or eight servings of gelato, depending on your ice cream maker and the amount of ingredients added to the base.

MAKING SORBETTO AT HOME

The sorbetto recipes also are very easy to make. Most contain just fruit and a simple syrup made with sugar and water (see page 118). Sometimes alcohol and other flavorings are added in keeping with the emphasis on bold and often surprising combinations. Sorbetti make the best use of seasonal produce, and Ciao Bella's recipes are loaded with it; the most common reaction to trying our sorbetti for the first time is, "It tastes just like fresh fruit." So will your results!

A NOTE ON INGREDIENTS

Gelato contains just the right amount of cream to give it a smooth texture and taste. Since it contains less cream than ice cream does, there's more room for the flavor to come through. And since gelato is already lower in fat than ice cream, don't use anything but whole milk; gelato made with lowfat milk will taste significantly less rich. The eggs also add to the richness of the custard and give it structure. Sugar provides both sweetness and texture. The more sugar the gelato contains, the slower it will freeze, and if there isn't enough sugar the result may be a bit icy. This goes for alcohol, too: Gelati made with alcohol won't freeze as solid and are best kept in the coldest part of the freezer.

Keeping all your ingredients as cold as possible helps guarantee the creamiest texture. It's even a good idea to keep the mixing bowls, whisk, and gelato canister in the refrigerator or freezer before you start making the recipe, if space allows. Also, freezing nuts and other mix-ins keeps them from getting soggy.

EQUIPMENT

Although hand-crank ice cream makers evoke a certain sense of nostalgia, you are much more likely to make your own gelato if you have an electric machine.

A countertop model containing a canister of refrigerant is the most affordable option, but the canister needs to be kept in the freezer for at least twenty-four hours before using, so advance planning is required (or if you have space, you can keep the canister in the freezer at the ready at all times). Unfortunately, the frozen canisters stay cold enough for churning only one batch of gelato at a time, though you can buy an extra canister if you'd like to be able to churn two batches in a day.

A continuous, compressor-type machine with a built-in refrigerating unit is the most convenient option—because there is no frozen canister involved, and you can make as many batches in any given day as you like. These machines are heavier—thirty pounds or so—plus they take up more counter space and are several times the price. Choose according to your needs; both machines will churn out a creamy, great-tasting gelato in the space of thirty to forty minutes.

Other tools you'll need to make your kitchen gelato- and sorbetto-ready:

- **WHISK:** for beating the eggs for the custard

- **WOODEN SPOON:** for stirring the custard

- **FLEXIBLE SPATULA (PREFERABLY SILICONE):** to scrape down the saucepan and bowl

- **CHEF'S KNIFE:** for chopping ingredients

- **MEASURING UTENSILS:** wet and dry measuring cups and measuring spoons

- **THERMOMETER:** for cooking the custard; see opposite

- **SEVERAL BOWLS:** for separating eggs, mixing ingredients, and making custard; include one heat-proof bowl

- **HEAVY-BOTTOM SAUCEPAN:** for even heat distribution for making the custard

- **BLENDER AND/OR FOOD PROCESSOR:** for turning fruit into puree for sorbetti

- **COFFEE GRINDER:** for making nut pastes

- **FINE-MESH STRAINER:** for straining the custard and separating seeds from fruit

- **STURDY PLASTIC PINT OR QUART CONTAINERS:** for storing gelato and sorbetto

- **ICE CREAM SCOOPER:** either a lever-type scooper with a quick-release handle, a spade-type scooper, or a round metal scoop with a defrosting liquid contained in the handle

Choosing a Thermometer

Temperature is a crucial factor in making a custard base, and your most accurate gauge is a food thermometer. There are three choices available:

CANDY THERMOMETER: Choose one with clear markings and a clip that allows it to be safely secured to the side of the pan. The thermometer will stay in the pan as the custard is coming up to temperature, so you'll know exactly when you've hit the right number.

INSTANT-READ THERMOMETER: It isn't kept in the pan as the custard is heating, so it doesn't get in the way of stirring. However, depending on the brand, it can take up to thirty seconds to give a reading, and you may have to check on it a few times.

NON-CONTACT INFRARED THERMOMETER: It quickly and conveniently measures the surface temperature of the liquid, providing fast temperature readings without physically touching the mixture. It safely measures the hot custard without risk of contamination and can provide several readings per second.

THE
BASICS

There's no better way to introduce you to the pleasures of making your own gelato than to start with the basics. First we present our Plain Base and Chocolate Base, which are the launching pads for most of our gelati; once you master the technique you'll be equipped to tackle the recipes that follow with ease. You can prepare the base a day ahead, then later pick a flavor to match your craving, mood, or dinner menu.

Our vanilla and chocolate gelati may be basic, but they just might be the best you've ever had—creamy, dense, and luxurious. And there are a surprising number of choices: vanilla from Madagascar or Tahiti, and chocolate from various countries or with different percentages of cacao, for example.

PLAIN BASE

This rich, custardy base is the starting point for many of the recipes that follow, spanning a range of flavors as familiar as maple walnut and as exotic as saffron spice or dulce de leche. But it's good enough to be made into gelato by itself, and in fact in Italy—where it is known as gelato de crema—it often is.

MAKES ENOUGH FOR ABOUT 1 QUART OF GELATO

2 cups whole milk

1 cup heavy cream

4 large egg yolks

⅔ cup sugar

In a heavy-bottom saucepan, combine the milk and cream. Place over medium-low heat and cook, stirring occasionally so a skin doesn't form, until tiny bubbles start to form around the edges and the mixture reaches a temperature of 170°F.

Meanwhile, in a medium heat-proof bowl, whisk the egg yolks until smooth. Gradually whisk in the sugar until it is well incorporated and the mixture is thick and pale yellow. Temper the egg yolks by very slowly pouring in the hot milk mixture while whisking continuously. Return the custard to the saucepan and place over low heat. Cook, stirring frequently with a wooden spoon, until the custard is thick enough to coat the back of the spoon and it reaches a temperature of 185°F. Do not bring to a boil.

Pour the mixture through a fine-mesh strainer into a clean bowl and let cool to room temperature, stirring every 5 minutes or so. To cool the custard quickly, make an ice bath by filling a large bowl with ice and water and placing the bowl with the custard in it; stir the custard until cooled. Once completely cooled, cover and refrigerate until very cold, at least 4 hours or overnight.

How to Temper Egg Yolks

Tempering gradually introduces a hot liquid to a cold one and brings the temperature of the two together. For the gelato bases the hot milk mixture is added to the egg yolks a little at a time so they are slowly brought up to a higher temperature. (If you were to add the egg yolks directly to the milk mixture, they would scramble.)

To temper, pour a small amount of the milk mixture into the egg yolks and sugar while whisking constantly. Add a little more milk while continuing to whisk, repeating the process until all of the milk mixture has been incorporated, then proceed with the recipe.

CHOCOLATE BASE

This intense chocolate foundation is good enough to stand up to the diverse chocolate-based recipes in this book, from Mexican Chocolate Gelato (page 103) to Chocolate Stout Gelato (page 113). After you've tried out some of our recipes, we encourage you to get creative and come up with your own signature chocolate gelato.

MAKES ENOUGH FOR
ABOUT 1 QUART OF GELATO

2 cups whole milk

1 cup heavy cream

½ cup unsweetened cocoa powder

4 ounces bittersweet chocolate
(about 60% cacao), finely
chopped

4 large egg yolks

¾ cup sugar

In a heavy-bottom saucepan, combine the milk and cream. Place over medium-low heat and cook, stirring occasionally so a skin doesn't form, until tiny bubbles start to form around the edges and the mixture reaches a temperature of 170°F. Turn off the heat and whisk in the cocoa powder. Add the chopped chocolate, and stir or whisk until the chocolate is completely melted and the mixture is smooth.

Meanwhile, in a medium heat-proof bowl, whisk the egg yolks until smooth. Gradually whisk in the sugar until it is well incorporated and the mixture is thick and pale yellow. Temper the egg yolks by very slowly pouring in the hot milk mixture, whisking continuously. Return the custard to the saucepan and place over low heat. Cook, stirring frequently with a wooden spoon, until the custard is thick enough to coat the back of the spoon and it reaches a temperature of 185°F. Do not bring to a boil.

Pour the mixture through a fine-mesh strainer into a clean bowl and cool to room temperature, stirring every 5 minutes or so. To cool the custard quickly, make an ice bath by filling a large bowl with ice and water and placing the bowl with the custard in it; stir the custard until cooled. Once completely cooled, cover and refrigerate until very cold, at least 4 hours or overnight.

MADAGASCAR BOURBON VANILLA GELATO

Vanilla is at its best in this gelato—lush and opulent and dotted with flecks of vanilla bean. It uses the same ingredients as our Plain Base (page 22) but with the addition of vanilla bean and pure vanilla extract.

We appreciate the intense, sweet flavor that Madagascar Bourbon vanilla lends to the gelato. It is the most widely available bean, and the Bourbon refers to Bourbon Island (now called Réunion Island), east of Madagascar, rather than to the whiskey. Photograph on page 4.

2 cups whole milk

1 cup heavy cream

½ Madagascar Bourbon vanilla bean

4 large egg yolks

⅔ cup sugar

¾ teaspoon pure Madagascar Bourbon vanilla extract

Pinch of salt

In a heavy-bottom saucepan, combine the milk and cream. Split the vanilla bean in half lengthwise and scrape the seeds from the bean into the cold milk and cream mixture. Save the pod for another use (see opposite).

Place the milk mixture over medium-low heat and cook, stirring occasionally so a skin doesn't form, until tiny bubbles start to form around the edges and the mixture reaches a temperature of 170°F. Remove the pan from the heat and set aside for 20 minutes to steep. Return the pan to the heat and bring the mixture back to 170°F.

Meanwhile, in a medium heat-proof bowl, whisk the egg yolks until smooth. Gradually whisk in the sugar until it is well incorporated and the mixture is thick and pale yellow. Temper the egg yolks by very slowly pouring in the hot milk mixture while whisking continuously. Return the custard to the saucepan and place over low heat. Cook, stirring frequently with a wooden spoon, until the custard is thick enough to coat the back of the spoon and it reaches a temperature of 185°F. Do not bring to a boil.

Pour the custard through a fine-mesh strainer into a clean bowl and cool to room temperature, stirring every 5 minutes or so. To cool the custard quickly, make an ice

bath by filling a large bowl with ice and water and placing the bowl with the custard in it; stir the custard until cooled. Once completely cooled, cover and refrigerate until very cold, at least 4 hours or overnight.

Remove the custard from the refrigerator and gently whisk in the vanilla extract and salt. Pour the mixture into the container of an ice cream machine and churn according to the manufacturer's instructions. Transfer to an airtight container and freeze for at least 2 hours before serving.

TAHITIAN VANILLA GELATO

In recent years Tahitian vanilla has become appreciated for its floral, almost musky but delicate flavor. Since these beans are produced in much smaller quantities than those from Madagascar, availability is sometimes limited (see Sources, page 174), and they can be a luxury item. Indulge when you can, as their complex taste profile is worth the splurge.

Follow the instructions for the Madagascar Bourbon Vanilla Gelato opposite, substituting ½ Tahitian vanilla bean for the Bourbon vanilla bean and using Tahitian vanilla extract. Use the entire vanilla bean for a deeper flavor.

Working with Vanilla Beans

To remove the seeds from a vanilla bean, place the bean on a cutting board and cut it in half lengthwise using the tip of a sharp paring knife. Following the length of the bean, use the blade of the knife to scrape out the seeds. Stash any leftover pods in a container of sugar and leave for a week or two to make vanilla sugar; it's great stirred into your coffee or sprinkled on berries or French toast.

CLASSIC CHOCOLATE GELATO

Chocolate perfection, pure and simple.

Ciao Bella Classic Chocolate Gelato is simply our deep Chocolate Base in its basic form; it stands alone in its sophisticated simplicity or can be used for infinite variations. Try experimenting with spice and different percentages of chocolate—milk chocolate for kids and dark and single-origin chocolates for chocolate connoisseurs. We recommend using a bittersweet chocolate with about 60% cacao for our chocolate recipes, but you could go up or down a bit according to your preference.

Chocolate Base (page 25)

Make the Chocolate Base and chill as directed.

Pour the custard into the container of an ice cream machine and churn according to the manufacturer's instructions. Transfer to an airtight container and freeze for at least 2 hours before serving.

CAYENNE CHOCOLATE GELATO

This increasingly popular flavor combination actually dates back to ancient Mexico, where the Maya and Aztecs created this pairing centuries ago. Add 1/8 teaspoon cayenne pepper, or to taste, to the Chocolate Base before churning. Remember that a little goes a long way; the idea is to emphasize the contrasting flavors, not to overpower with spice. Try a variety of chiles—chipotles for a smoky touch or ancho chiles for a milder, fruity flavor.

DARK CHOCOLATE GELATO

Use a chocolate with 70% cacao in the Chocolate Base. You might want to try Valrhona, a strong, full-bodied chocolate with a hint of tartness that is a favorite of French pastry chefs. Increase the amount of chocolate—up to 6 ounces—for the ultimate chocolate experience.

MILK CHOCOLATE GELATO

Use milk chocolate in the Chocolate Base and reduce the amount of sugar to 1/2 cup and the cocoa powder to 1/4 cup for a lighter chocolate; it's great as a base for children's favorites such as Chocolate S'mores Gelato (page 79).

Single-Origin Chocolate

We choose coffee and wine based on their region, and now connoisseurs choose chocolate the same way. Chocolate lovers have become interested in where their chocolate comes from, and single-origin chocolate allows us to appreciate the subtle nuances that arise from one specific region rather than from blends. You also benefit from the ability to know how it is grown and how fairly the cocoa bean pickers are treated. For more on responsible companies that use fair trade practices, see opposite.

Chef Danilo recommends trying Puertomar chocolate from Domori, an Italian company that sources its chocolate from Venezuela using a very high-quality cacao that has been selected and roasted in small batches. Although the chocolate has a high percentage of cacao, it is surprisingly sweet and smooth, and its complex flavor profile includes notes of fruit, cream, and nuts. Just substitute the Puertomar chocolate for the regular bittersweet chocolate in the Classic Chocolate Gelato (page 28) recipe; you'll need four 25-gram (.88-ounce) packages of Puertomar 75% extra bitter (see Sources, page 174).

Chef Danilo's Single-Origin Chocolate Picks
(see Sources, page 174)

From Venezuela:
Apamate dark chocolate (73.5%) from El Rey; earthy, slightly spicy, and smooth
Gran Saman dark chocolate (70%) from El Rey; intense, complex, and bitter

From Ecuador:
Los Rios organic dark chocolate (72%) from Pacari; strong cacao with notes of fruit and coffee

From Africa:
Pure dark chocolate (75%) from Claudio Corallo; medium body and firm; floral and nutty flavors with a touch of cherry

Natural and Fair Chocolate

We went to our local chocolate expert, Sarah Endline, head of sweetriot chocolate company, to enlighten us on just what goes into the chocolate that we find on our grocery shelves. Sweetriot, based in New York City, is working to create a "sweet movement to fix the world" by engaging in an honest partnership with chocolate growers—from start to finish—to produce the all-natural chocolate that goes into their chocolate-covered cacao nibs and chocolate bars.

Sarah explains that what most people don't know is that chocolate comes from a fruit, not a factory. Most of the cacao beans grown in the world are exported from their country of origin to countries of manufacture, thus giving places such as Belgium and Switzerland their reputation for producing fine chocolate. But the truth is that chocolate starts twenty degrees north or south of the equator—primarily in Africa, Latin America, and the Caribbean.

Cacao grows in podlike fruits on the cacao tree. This is the raw material for the chocolate that ends up in the bars that we all enjoy. Preparing the cacao for processing is very labor intensive. It begins with harvesting the cacao beans: workers sit with buckets and piles of the fruits, and one by one crack open their hard shells with a machete. Inside is what people call the bean, but it's really the seed of the fruit covered with white pulp. The fruit and all cacao beans inside are pulled out and put straight into a fermenting bin for at least twenty-four hours; then the fruit and beans are dried in the sun.

Now the cacao beans are ready to go to a factory, where they are roasted, shelled to turn them into nibs, then ground to make chocolate paste—the base for chocolate bars. This is where the "locally grown" part of the process often ends. Fair trade chocolate has to do with paying the farmers equitably, but there is no stamp that lets you know whether the chocolate was processed in the country of origin.

Sweetriot chocolate takes people all the way back to the nib, and we've come up with two fantastic gelato recipes showcasing sweetriot's premium chocolate-covered cacao nibs.

CACAO NIB GELATO

Crunchy, intensely chocolaty cacao nibs are a great addition to just about any gelato. Here they provide a distinct flavor and texture contrast to our pure Plain Base. If you use sweetriot cacao nibs, you have a choice of 50%, 65%, or 70% dark chocolate (see Sources, page 174, for where to find them).

Plain Base (page 22)

¾ teaspoon pure vanilla extract

2 ounces (¼ cup) chocolate-covered cacao nibs, frozen

Make the Plain Base and chill as directed.

Gently whisk the vanilla into the base. Pour the mixture into the container of an ice cream machine and churn according to the manufacturer's instructions. Add the cacao nibs to the gelato 5 minutes before the churning is completed.

Transfer to an airtight container and freeze for at least 2 hours before serving.

CHOCOLATE CACAO NIB GELATO

Bittersweet chocolate and chocolate-covered cacao nibs—two layers of chocolate flavor—go into this luxurious gelato. We recommend using sweetriot's unBar; you'll need three 1.34-ounce bars (see Sources, page 174).

2 cups whole milk

1 cup heavy cream

½ cup unsweetened cocoa powder

4 egg yolks

¾ cup sugar

4 ounces bittersweet chocolate with cacao nibs, finely chopped

2 tablespoons chocolate-covered cacao nibs, frozen (optional)

In a heavy-bottom saucepan, combine the milk and cream. Place over medium-low heat and heat until tiny bubbles start to form around the edges and the mixture reaches a temperature of 170°F, stirring occasionally so a skin doesn't form. Turn off the heat and whisk in the cocoa powder until the mixture is smooth.

Meanwhile, in a medium heat-proof bowl, whisk the egg yolks until smooth. Gradually whisk in the sugar until it is well incorporated and the mixture is thick and pale yellow. Temper the egg yolks by very slowly pouring in the hot milk mixture, whisking continuously. Return the custard to the

SARAH ENDLINE's definition of real chocolate: "Chocolate that's high in cacao and natural, with a short ingredient list that has no unrecognizable ingredients."

saucepan and place over low heat. Heat, stirring frequently with a wooden spoon, until the custard is thick enough to coat the back of the spoon and it reaches a temperature of 185°F. Do not bring to a boil.

While the custard is heating, place the chopped chocolate in a heat-proof bowl. Set the bowl over a pan of barely simmering water; the bowl should be just above the water, not touching it. Stir until almost all the chocolate is melted; the last bits of chocolate will melt just by stirring.

Pour the custard through a fine-mesh strainer into a clean bowl, then whisk in the warm melted chocolate until fully incorporated. Cool completely, stirring often. To cool the custard quickly, make an ice bath by filling a large bowl with ice and water and placing the bowl with the custard in it. Once completely cooled, cover and refrigerate until very cold, at least 4 hours or overnight.

Pour the custard into the container of an ice cream machine and churn according to the manufacturer's instructions. Add the cacao nibs, if using, to the gelato 5 minutes before the churning is completed. Transfer to an airtight container and freeze for at least 2 hours before serving.

WHITE CHOCOLATE GELATO

Despite its silky texture, white chocolate is not chocolate at all, according to the Food and Drug Administration (and any chocolatier worth his or her salt), because even though it usually contains cocoa butter, it does not contain chocolate liquor (the liquid form of chocolate that contains both cocoa butter and cocoa solids). Chocolate or not, White Chocolate Gelato stands on its own merits—sweet, creamy, and irresistible.

2 cups whole milk

1 cup heavy cream

6 ounces white chocolate, finely chopped

4 large egg yolks

¼ cup sugar

In a heavy-bottom saucepan, combine the milk and cream. Place over medium-low heat and cook, stirring occasionally so a skin doesn't form, until tiny bubbles start to form around the edges and the mixture reaches a temperature of 170°F. Turn off the heat and add the white chocolate; stir or whisk until the mixture is smooth.

Meanwhile, in a medium heat-proof bowl, whisk the egg yolks until smooth. Gradually whisk in the sugar until it is well incorporated and the mixture is thick and pale yellow. Temper the egg yolks by very slowly pouring in the hot milk mixture while whisking continuously. Return the custard to the saucepan and place over low heat. Cook, stirring frequently with a wooden spoon, until the custard is thick enough to coat the back of the spoon and it reaches a temperature of 185°F. Do not bring to a boil.

Pour the custard through a fine-mesh strainer into a clean bowl and cool completely, stirring often. To cool the custard quickly, make an ice bath by filling a large bowl with ice and water and placing the bowl with the custard in it; stir the custard until cooled. Once completely cooled, cover and refrigerate until very cold, at least 4 hours or overnight.

Pour the custard into the container of an ice cream machine and churn according to the manufacturer's instructions. Transfer to an airtight container and freeze for at least 2 hours before serving.

ITALIAN CLASSICS

Some Italians go out for gelato almost every day. But you won't find them running to the store for a pint; eating gelato is a social experience, and practically every town has at least one local gelateria where everything is homemade and *artiginale*, or "artisanal." This is the place to meet up, enjoy a gelato after dinner, or take a mid-afternoon gelato break, perhaps with an espresso on the side.

With the exception of a few larger shops, most Italian gelaterie don't offer a wide variety of flavors. The objective is not to reinvent gelato but rather to re-create the traditional flavors of one's grandparents—and many of the recipes have been passed down from one generation to the next, frequently using local ingredients. Almost every neighborhood gelato shop offers a selection of some of the classics. Staying true to the Italian roots of this frozen dessert, Ciao Bella's most popular flavors have included hazelnut, gianduja, bacio, and pistachio, which are featured in this section, along with several other timeless varieties. But in true Ciao Bella fashion, we have also added a few unique twists to the classics, such as the option of swirling caramel into your Cinnamon Gelato or brownies to your Pistachio Gelato. And we include a couple of slightly untraditional but standout flavors: Prune and Armagnac, and Fig and Port.

RISO GELATO

Riso, the Italian version of rice pudding, originated in the north of Italy. When times were tough people made do with what they had—and if nothing else, every Italian family would have rice in the house. With a little creativity, this inexpensive, easy-to-make but satisfying dessert was born. In gelato form the rice gives a bit of structure to the ultra-creamy base—comfort food with a bit of decadence. You can serve it with any type of fresh fruit or sprinkle with raisins and walnuts.

Plain Base (page 22)

½ cup Arborio rice

3 cups whole milk

¼ cup sugar

¼ teaspoon ground cinnamon

Pinch of ground cloves

⅛ teaspoon pure vanilla extract

Make the Plain Base and chill as directed.

Bring a medium saucepan of enough water to cover the rice to a boil. Add the rice, return to a boil, then reduce the heat and cook, uncovered, at a low boil until the rice is fairly soft with just a little bite remaining, about 20 minutes. Drain.

Combine the milk, sugar, cinnamon, and cloves in the pan the rice cooked in, and whisk to dissolve the sugar and spices. Place over medium heat and bring just to a simmer. Add the rice, return to a simmer, and cook, uncovered, until the rice is quite soft but still whole, about 30 minutes. Transfer the rice mixture to a heat-proof bowl, stirring as it cools to keep it from sticking together and to prevent a skin from forming. Transfer the rice to a bowl and cool completely. Cover the rice and refrigerate until cold, about 2 hours.

Remove the rice from the refrigerator. Gently whisk the vanilla into the base, then stir in the rice. Pour the mixture into the container of an ice cream machine and churn according to the manufacturer's instructions. Transfer to an airtight container and freeze for at least 2 hours before serving.

HAZELNUT (*NOCCIOLA*) GELATO

Hazelnut, or *nocciola,* is the quintessential Italian flavor. It makes its way into countless desserts, none more popular than gelato. The traditional version is smooth, but if you like yours crunchy, add ½ cup frozen chopped roasted hazelnuts during the last 5 minutes of churning. For an even more untraditional take, see the recipe for Hazelnut Biscotti Gelato on page 78.

At Ciao Bella we favor Tonda Gentile delle Langhe hazelnuts from the Piedmont region of Italy, considered the best in the world and recognized by chefs and the confectionery industry for their rich, superior flavor. They are the nut of choice for Italy's many chocolate-hazelnut sweets.

Plain Base (page 22)

½ cup roasted hazelnuts (see page 47), cooled and ground into a paste in a coffee grinder

Make the Plain Base and chill as directed.

In a blender, combine the hazelnut paste with half of the base and blend until fully incorporated. Whisk into the remaining base, pour into the container of an ice cream machine, and churn according to the manufacturer's instructions. Transfer to an airtight container and freeze for at least 2 hours before serving.

bacio

gianduja

GIANDUJA GELATO

Gianduja is a delectable combination of sweet milk chocolate and hazelnuts—a match made in Italian heaven. It was born out of a time of scarcity during the Napoleonic Wars in the 1800s, when cocoa was rationed and hazelnuts were blended with chocolate to extend it. The name *gianduja* comes from *Gioan d'la duja,* a mask from Torino's Carnevale celebration representing a simple man from the country with an inclination for the sensual pleasures of life. The quality of the gianduja depends on the hazelnuts; the best gianduja uses hazelnuts from the Piedmont region of Italy. Nutella is the spreadable version of gianduja.

2 cups whole milk

1 cup heavy cream

6 ounces gianduja chocolate (see Sources, page 174), finely chopped

4 egg yolks

½ cup sugar

In a heavy-bottom saucepan, combine the milk and cream. Place over medium-low heat and cook, stirring occasionally so a skin doesn't form, until tiny bubbles start to form around the edges and the mixture reaches a temperature of 170°F. Turn off the heat and add the chopped chocolate; stir or whisk until the chocolate is completely melted and the mixture is smooth.

Meanwhile, in a medium heat-proof bowl, whisk the egg yolks until smooth. Gradually whisk in the sugar until it is well incorporated and the mixture is thick and pale yellow. Temper the egg yolks by very slowly pouring in the hot milk mixture while whisking continuously. Return the custard to the saucepan and place over low heat. Cook, stirring frequently with a wooden spoon, until the custard is thick enough to coat the back of the spoon and it reaches a temperature of 185°F. Do not bring to a boil.

Pour the custard through a fine-mesh strainer into a clean bowl and cool completely, stirring every 5 minutes or so. To cool the custard quickly, make an ice bath by filling a large bowl with ice and water and placing the bowl with the custard in it; stir the custard until cooled. Once completely cooled, cover and refrigerate until very cold, at least 4 hours or overnight.

Pour the custard into the container of an ice cream machine and churn according to the manufacturer's instructions. Transfer to an airtight container and freeze for at least 2 hours before serving.

BACIO GELATO

Bacio, Italian for "kiss," is the same combination of chocolate and hazelnut as gianduja but made with bittersweet chocolate. It is based on the famous Baci hazelnut-filled chocolate candy kisses, which date back to 1922 when Luisa Spagnoli, a confectioner at the Perugina chocolate factory, was having a clandestine affair with the company's heir Giovanni Buitoni. Spagnoli would wrap love notes around the chocolates as a way of communicating her secret love to Buitoni. Their romance was immortalized in Baci chocolates, and to this day you'll find a poetic love note included with every chocolate kiss. Pairing this gelato with its lighter cousin makes for an indulgent combination; see photograph on page 40.

Chocolate Base (page 25)

½ cup roasted hazelnuts (see page 47), cooled and ground into a paste in a coffee grinder

½ teaspoon pure vanilla extract

½ cup chopped roasted hazelnuts (see page 47), frozen

Make the Chocolate Base and chill as directed.

In a blender, combine the hazelnut paste and vanilla with half of the base and blend until fully incorporated. Whisk into the remaining base, pour into the container of an ice cream machine, and churn according to the manufacturer's instructions. Add the chopped hazelnuts 5 minutes before the churning is completed. Transfer to an airtight container and freeze for at least 2 hours before serving.

Torino is also famous for *bicerin,* a traditional hot drink made of espresso, drinking chocolate, and milk served in layers in a small rounded glass. The word *bicerin* is Piedmontese for "small glass" and this drink is recognizable by its distinct layers. You'll find it in just about every bar and restaurant in the region; it makes a rich intermezzo or end to a meal.

PRUNE AND ARMAGNAC GELATO

Armagnac—a fine French brandy with a delicate, woody flavor and notes of chocolate—adds sophistication to the demure but flavorful prunes in this classic French pairing. It's a bit more subtle than the Fig and Port Gelato (page 61), and the sweet prunes give it an extra-creamy texture. You can substitute cognac if that's what you have on hand. Note that the prunes need twelve hours to macerate, so plan ahead.

1 cup pitted prunes

1 cup Armagnac (or any good brandy)

Plain Base (page 22)

Place the prunes and Armagnac in a medium bowl. Cover lightly with a clean kitchen towel and set aside for 12 hours at room temperature to macerate.

Make the Plain Base and chill as directed.

Strain the prunes from the Armagnac, reserving it to serve alongside the gelato. Chop half of the prunes into small bits or big pieces—whatever your preference—and place them in the refrigerator to chill.

Place the remaining prunes in a blender and add half of the base. Blend until fully incorporated, then whisk into the remaining base. Pour the mixture into the container of an ice cream machine and churn according to the manufacturer's instructions. Add the chopped prunes 5 minutes before the churning is completed. Transfer to an airtight container and freeze for at least 2 hours before serving.

"TO MAKE Ciao Bella's gelato the best there is, we combine classic methods of Old World gelato production with a modern sense of experimentation and taste. I would be proud to serve our gelato in Torino at my family's dinner table—and that's saying something!"
—CHEF DANILO

STRACCIATELLA GELATO

Stracciatella means "torn apart" in Italian. Melted chocolate is drizzled over just-churned vanilla gelato and quickly mixed in, creating a chocolate ribbon, parts of which will tear apart and delightfully melt in your mouth along with the gelato. This is Italy's precursor to chocolate chip ice cream. Making Stracciatella Gelato at home is particularly rewarding, as the method of mixing in the chocolate by hand is something that just can't be done on a commercial scale.

Plain Base (page 22)

¼ teaspoon pure vanilla extract

2 ounces bittersweet chocolate, finely chopped

Make the Plain Base and chill as directed.

Gently whisk the vanilla into the base. Pour the mixture into the container of an ice cream machine and churn according to the manufacturer's instructions.

While the gelato is churning, place the chocolate in a heat-proof bowl. Set the bowl over a pan of barely simmering water; the bottom of the bowl should be just above the water, not touching it. Stir until just melted. You're working with a small amount of chocolate, so it will take only a few minutes to melt. Watch closely so it doesn't overheat, which can cause the chocolate to break up and start to burn. Remove from the heat and cool until just warm, not hot (about 100°F). Alternatively you can melt the chocolate in the microwave: Place the chocolate in a microwave-safe bowl and heat on high power for 20 seconds, then stir. Repeat once or twice as needed until almost all the chocolate is melted; the last bits of chocolate will melt just by stirring.

Just after the gelato is churned, drizzle the melted chocolate in a thin stream over the top and using a rubber spatula quickly fold it into the gelato to create ribbons of chocolate. Alternatively, drizzle the chocolate into the gelato 2 minutes before the churning is completed.

Transfer to an airtight container and freeze for at least 2 hours before serving.

WHEN TRAVELING IN ITALY, to be sure your gelato is the real thing: Look for signs that read *produzione propria* ("our own production"), or *gelato artiginale* ("artisanal gelato").

PISTACHIO GELATO

This is one of my favorite flavors, and while I was in Italy I would go from gelateria to gelateria to sample the various versions. We at Ciao Bella use Bronte pistachios from Sicily, which are absolutely the best in the world; they are a striking green color and have an intense, grassy aroma from the mineral-rich volcanic soil they're grown in. You can use either salted or unsalted pistachios in this gelato. —FW

Plain Base (page 22)

½ cup shelled roasted pistachios (see below), cooled and ground into a paste in a coffee grinder

⅛ teaspoon pure almond extract

½ cup shelled roasted pistachios

Make the Plain Base and chill as directed.

In a blender, combine the pistachio paste and almond extract with half of the base. Blend until smooth, then whisk into the remaining base. Pour the mixture into the container of an ice cream machine and churn according to the manufacturer's instructions. Add the whole pistachios 5 minutes before the churning is completed. Transfer to an airtight container and freeze for at least 2 hours before serving.

Roasting Nuts

Preheat the oven to 350°F.

Spread the nuts on a rimmed baking sheet in a single layer. Place the baking sheet in the oven, and roast for 10 to 15 minutes, stirring once or twice, until the nuts are fragrant and lightly browned. Remove from the oven, transfer to a plate, and cool.

For hazelnuts, roast for 10 to 15 minutes, stirring once or twice, until the skins are lightly browned and start to crack. Remove from the oven and immediately wrap in a clean kitchen towel. Leave for 1 minute to steam, then rub the hazelnuts in the towel to loosen and remove the skins. (It's fine if some of the skins don't rub off.) Cool completely before using.

PISTACHIO BROWNIE GELATO

To make this kid-friendly take, cut ½ cup to 1 cup frozen brownies into small pieces to use as an accent, or break them into chunks large enough to sink your teeth into. Stir the brownie pieces into the Pistachio Gelato just after churning. The brownies from the recipe on page 49 are so fudgy that they can be hard to cut; to make things easier, cut off a large square and freeze it before chopping.

ELENI'S FUDGY WALNUT BROWNIES

Pistachio Gelato steps up a few notches with Eleni Gianopulos's richest-ever Fudgy Walnut Brownies. Eleni's New York, a bakery located in the Chelsea Market, is famous for the owner's hand-iced cookies, particularly her Hollywood line, which turns the faces of Oscar nominees into edible art.

Eleni and Ciao Bella have partnered to create several treats, including Cinnamon with Oatmeal Cookie Gelato (page 80) and the Ottimo gelato sandwich (see page 168); here Eleni has graciously shared the recipe for her wildly popular brownies. They are also available at her New York bakery; and an equally delicious version is available by mail order (see Sources, page 174). You'll have plenty of brownies left over, so serve them alongside the gelato or keep them on hand in the freezer.

MAKES TWENTY-FOUR 2-INCH BROWNIES

1 cup (2 sticks) unsalted butter

One 12-ounce bag semisweet chocolate chips

1 cup all-purpose flour

¼ cup unsweetened cocoa powder

½ teaspoon salt

4 large eggs

1½ cups sugar

1 cup chopped walnuts

Preheat the oven to 350°F and grease a 9 by 13-inch baking pan with cooking spray.

In a small saucepan, melt the butter over low heat. Reserve ½ cup of the chocolate chips and add the remaining chocolate chips to the melted butter. Stir until the chips are completely melted and the mixture is smooth. Remove from the heat and cool slightly.

Sift the flour and cocoa powder into a medium bowl. Add the salt and stir to combine.

Place the eggs in the bowl of an electric mixer and beat on low speed using the whisk attachment until smooth. Gradually add the sugar until incorporated; increase the speed to medium high and beat for 2 to 3 minutes, until the mixture is pale and thick. Turn the speed down to low and gradually add the reserved chocolate and butter mixture. Scrape down the sides of the bowl and beat until smooth. Add the flour and cocoa mixture, and mix just until combined. Add the walnuts and remaining chocolate chips and mix just to combine.

Pour the batter into the prepared pan and bake for about 25 minutes, until a toothpick inserted in the center comes out with a few wet crumbs. Remove from the oven, place on a wire rack, and cool completely before cutting.

COFFEE GELATO

Italians have a passion for coffee, and the selection, blending, and roasting of the beans is what makes Italy the master of the coffee industry. Creamy, aromatic, humming with flavor, and with notes of cinnamon and tobacco, this gelato is great for those who dare to do as the Italians do and eat gelato for breakfast. By using your favorite beans, type of roast, decaf versus caffeinated—you can create your own personal coffee gelato experience.

Plain Base (page 22)

2 teaspoons instant coffee granules, finely ground

Make the Plain Base and chill as directed.

Gently whisk the coffee granules into the base until completely dissolved. Pour the mixture into the container of an ice cream machine and churn according to the manufacturer's instructions. Transfer to an airtight container and freeze for at least 2 hours before serving.

Using Instant Coffee in Gelato

In our coffee gelati we call for finely grinding the instant coffee granules so they dissolve easily into the base. If you don't have a coffee grinder, you can blend the coffee granules with half of the base, then whisk into the remaining base. Or easier still, you could add the instant coffee granules to the custard while it's still hot and stir until dissolved.

mocha chip

espresso

ESPRESSO GELATO

This is the strongest of the coffee gelati; its pure coffee energy goes right to the point. (Late-night indulgences can keep you up, so be careful!) Photograph on page 51.

Plain Base (page 22)

½ cup whole milk

3 tablespoons plus 1 teaspoon very finely ground espresso beans

2 teaspoons finely ground instant coffee granules

Make the Plain Base and chill as directed.

In a small saucepan, combine the milk and 3 tablespoons of the espresso powder. Place over medium heat and bring just to a simmer. Remove from the heat and set aside to steep for 20 minutes. Pour the milk mixture through a fine-mesh strainer into a bowl, pressing on the solids to extract all the liquid. Add the instant coffee granules and stir until dissolved. Refrigerate until cold, at least 30 minutes.

Gently whisk the milk mixture into the base, then whisk in the remaining 1 teaspoon espresso powder. Pour the custard into the container of an ice cream machine and churn according to the manufacturer's instructions. Transfer to an airtight container and freeze for at least 2 hours before serving.

MOCHA CHIP GELATO

Coffee and chocolate—the best of two worlds—come together in this dense, indulgent gelato. Basically, it's a variant of caffè latte with the addition of chocolate. Photograph on page 51.

Chocolate Base (page 25)

2 teaspoons finely ground instant coffee granules

½ teaspoon finely ground coffee beans

2 ounces coarsely chopped bittersweet chocolate (about 60%), frozen

Make the Chocolate Base and chill as directed.

Gently whisk the coffee granules and ground coffee beans into the base until dissolved. Pour the mixture into the container of an ice cream machine and churn according to the manufacturer's instructions. Add the chopped chocolate 5 minutes before the churning is completed. Transfer to an airtight container and freeze for at least 2 hours before serving.

> **ESPRESSO IS TO ITALY** what Champagne is to France.
> —CHARLES-MAURICE DE TALLEYRAND-PÉRIGORD (1754–1838), FRENCH DIPLOMAT

CARAMEL GELATO

This irresistibly sweet and creamy gelato is one of the more common flavors in Italian gelaterie. In Italy it's usually served without the swirl of caramel; here we give you the choice. Photograph on page 54.

Plain Base (page 22)

¼ cup Caramel Sauce (page 55), at room temperature

Make the Plain Base and chill as directed.

Gently whisk the caramel sauce into the base. Pour the mixture into the container of an ice cream machine and churn according to the manufacturer's instructions. Transfer to an airtight container and freeze for at least 2 hours before serving.

CARAMEL SWIRL GELATO

Make the Caramel Gelato above. Just after churning, gradually squeeze an additional ½ cup of Caramel Sauce from a squeeze bottle over the top and quickly and lightly swirl in a zigzag pattern with a spoon or butter knife. Alternatively, transfer one-third of the gelato to the container you'll be freezing it in and squeeze 2 tablespoons of the additional caramel sauce over it. Repeat layering with the remaining gelato and caramel, then freeze for at least 2 hours before serving.

CARAMEL SAUCE

With its hypnotically smoky-sweet flavor and silky texture, this caramel sauce accentuates anything it's added to. That's why you'll see it used many times over in Ciao Bella recipes, and we encourage you to swirl some caramel into any of your favorites. We've also come up with a couple of gelati using caramels from the southern hemisphere that you can try: Dulce de Leche Gelato (page 105), a South American–style caramel, and Banana Cajeta Cashew Gelato (page 92), made with a goat's milk caramel from Mexico.

The sauce will keep for about ten days and you can easily double this recipe. There are many ways to use any remaining caramel: drizzled over fresh fruit, whisked into a cup of warm milk, or stirred into coffee instead of the usual spoonful of sugar, to name just a few. Make sure to use a large saucepan to prevent the caramel from boiling over, which could cause a sticky mess.

MAKES ABOUT 1 CUP

½ cup sugar

1 cup heavy cream

In a large, dry heavy-bottom saucepan, heat the sugar over medium heat undisturbed until it begins to melt, then stir constantly with a wooden spoon until it's completely melted and turns a reddish-brown color, about 10 minutes. If the sugar starts to bubble vigorously and rise up the pan, quickly remove from the heat and stir until it comes down.

Lower the heat and carefully add ½ cup of the cream (you may want to keep a distance from the pan, as the mixture will steam and bubble vigorously). Stir until the cream is completely incorporated, then stir in the remaining ½ cup cream. Cook, whisking, until the sauce is thickened but still pourable (it will continue to thicken as it cools), about 10 minutes. (Any time the caramel starts to rise up the pan, remove from the heat and stir until it comes down.) Cool completely, then refrigerate.

Bring the caramel to room temperature before using. If it becomes too firm to pour, gently rewarm over medium-low heat, then let cool to room temperature before swirling, or drizzle it warm over gelato as a topping.

CINNAMON GELATO

Cinnamon is the solo act in this sophisticated but simple gelato. Make sure to use fresh cinnamon (replace your jar if you've had it for more than six months) to take full advantage of its sweet, warming flavor and aroma. We favor cinnamon from Indonesia for its intense red color and delicate flavor, but slightly sweet Ceylon cinnamon (also known as "true" cinnamon) or the stronger Cassia cinnamon, which you'll often find just labeled as "cinnamon" in this country, will also work well.

Though perfectly delicious on its own, Cinnamon Gelato pairs well with all things sweet—drizzled with honey or served atop a slice of warm apple tart, for example. For a particularly American experience, try a scoop over pumpkin pie or partner it with Pumpkin and Spice Gelato (page 75). Cinnamon also provides the canvas for one of Ciao Bella's all-time favorites, Cinnamon with Oatmeal Cookie Gelato (page 80).

Plain Base (page 22)

¼ teaspoon pure vanilla extract

2 teaspoons ground cinnamon

Make the Plain Base and chill as directed.

Gently whisk the vanilla and cinnamon into the base. Pour the mixture into the container of an ice cream machine and churn according to the manufacturer's instructions. Transfer to an airtight container and freeze for at least 2 hours before serving.

CINNAMON WITH CARAMEL SWIRL GELATO

The caramel has a positively explosive effect on the cinnamon; your taste buds won't know what hit them.

Make the Cinnamon Gelato above. Just after churning, gradually squeeze ½ cup of Caramel Sauce (page 55) from a squeeze bottle over the top and quickly and lightly swirl in a zigzag pattern with a spoon or butter knife. Alternatively, transfer one third of the gelato to the container you'll be freezing it in and squeeze 2 tablespoons of the caramel over it. Repeat layering with the remaining gelato and caramel, then freeze for at least 2 hours before serving.

ZABAIONE GELATO

Zabaione, a luxurious but straightforward dessert made with three ingredients—egg yolks, sugar, and Marsala wine—is familiar to everyone in Italy. (In America it's usually spelled *zabaglione*; and the French version is *sabayon*.) It can be served either cold or warm—made tableside—and is also a great accompanying sauce for cakes. Every Italian grandmother knows to give it to her grandchildren in the winter when they're looking a little under the weather—and every child gladly takes to this sweet remedy.

Fresh strawberries or raspberries are the topping of choice for this gelato, or try adding strawberries directly to the base (opposite). Chocolate lovers won't go wrong by crumbling in frozen chocolate cookies at the end of churning or by topping their bowl of gelato with shaved bittersweet chocolate.

2 cups whole milk

2 cups heavy cream

2 teaspoons grated lemon zest

6 egg yolks

⅔ cup sugar

Pinch of salt

2 tablespoons Marsala wine

In a heavy-bottom saucepan, combine the milk, cream, and lemon zest. Place over medium-low heat and cook, stirring occasionally so a skin doesn't form, until tiny bubbles start to form around the edges and the mixture reaches a temperature of 170°F.

Meanwhile, in a medium heat-proof bowl, whisk the egg yolks until smooth. Gradually whisk in the sugar until it is well incorporated and the mixture is thick and pale yellow. Whisk in the salt. Temper the egg yolks by very slowly pouring in the hot milk mixture while whisking continuously.

Pour the custard through a fine-mesh strainer into a clean bowl, whisk in the wine, and cool completely, stirring often. To cool the custard quickly, make an ice bath by filling a large bowl with ice and water and placing the bowl with the custard in it; stir the custard until cooled. Once completely cooled, cover and refrigerate until very cold, at least 4 hours or overnight.

Pour the custard into the container of an ice cream machine and churn according to the manufacturer's instructions. Transfer to an airtight container and freeze for at least 2 hours before serving.

EGGNOG GELATO
Substitute 2 tablespoons rum for the Marsala wine and add a pinch of ground nutmeg. This turns a classic Italian dessert into a traditional American holiday treat.

STRAWBERRY
ZABAIONE GELATO

Prepare the base for the Zabaione Gelato opposite. Hull and thinly slice ½ pound strawberries (about 1 pint) and place in a large bowl. Sprinkle with 2 tablespoons sugar, then add 1 tablespoon fresh lemon juice. Toss until the sugar is dissolved and the strawberries are well coated. Cover and refrigerate, tossing occasionally, for at least 2 hours or overnight to macerate. Gently stir the strawberries into the zabaione custard and churn according to the manufacturer's instructions. Transfer to an airtight container and freeze for at least 2 hours before serving.

FIG AND PORT GELATO

This Mediterranean-inspired gelato has a fairly assertive kick provided by the port. Cooking the figs in the fruity fortified wine intensifies their inherent sweetness.

Plain Base (page 22)

1 cup ruby port

2 teaspoons honey

1 cup finely chopped dried figs

Make the Plain Base and chill as directed.

Pour ¾ cup of the port into a medium saucepan; add the honey and whisk until dissolved. Add the figs and place over medium heat. Bring to a simmer and cook, stirring often, until the wine is absorbed and the figs start to caramelize, 10 to 15 minutes. Remove from the heat and let cool completely.

Transfer half of the caramelized figs to a food processor and puree until smooth. Place the pureed figs and chopped figs in separate containers, cover, and refrigerate until very cold.

Gently whisk the pureed figs and remaining ¼ cup port into the base. Pour the mixture into the container of an ice cream machine and churn according to the manufacturer's instructions. Add the chopped figs 5 minutes before the churning is completed. Transfer to an airtight container and freeze for at least 2 hours before serving.

AMERICAN FAVORITES

In this section we combine classic Italian gelato-making techniques and quintessential American flavors such as blueberry and strawberry. The strawberry variation with a swirl of balsamic syrup is one great example not to be missed; it also showcases how Ciao Bella adds ingredients favored by the country's top chefs. Recipes reminiscent of particularly American desserts such as apple pie (Apple Caramel Crisp Gelato) and pumpkin pie (Pumpkin and Spice Gelato) flatter the fall season.

We've included gelati inspired by regional ingredients, such as pecans from the South (Butter Pecan Gelato), maple from New England (Maple Walnut Gelato and Maple Gingersnap Gelato), Key limes from Florida (Key Lime with Graham Cracker Gelato), and pralines from New Orleans (Banana with Walnut Praline Gelato).

The section ends with an assortment of gelati especially for kids; they will be excited about our fanciful cookie- and candy-inspired flavors, such as Cookies and Cream, Chocolate S'mores, and Malted Milk Ball. And nothing says comfort food more than Peanut Butter with Strawberry Swirl Gelato: It's a whole new take on "PB & J."

STRAWBERRY GELATO

There's no better way to capture the flavor of summer than with a berry gelato. Here the strawberries are macerated and slightly caramelized to bring out their intrinsic sweetness.

Plain Base (page 22), with the amount of sugar reduced to ½ cup

1 pound strawberries (about 1 quart), hulled and thinly sliced

¼ cup sugar

2 tablespoons fresh lemon juice

Make the Plain Base and chill as directed.

Place the strawberries in a medium saucepan. Sprinkle with the sugar, then add the lemon juice; toss until the sugar is dissolved and the strawberries are well coated. Let sit for 15 minutes, stirring occasionally.

Place the pan of strawberries over medium-low heat and cook until the strawberries soften completely and the syrup just starts to thicken, about 10 minutes. Remove from the heat and let cool to room temperature. Transfer to a container, cover, and refrigerate until cold, at least 2 hours. (The strawberries may be prepared a day ahead.)

Reserve a quarter of the strawberries and syrup. Place the remaining strawberries in a blender or food processor, add half of the base, and blend until fully incorporated. Whisk into the remaining base.

Pour the mixture into the container of an ice cream machine and churn according to the manufacturer's instructions. Add the reserved strawberries 5 minutes before the churning is completed. Transfer to an airtight container and freeze for at least 2 hours before serving.

STRAWBERRY GELATO WITH BALSAMIC SWIRL

This one is a real attention-getter. The balsamic vinegar syrup (see page 66) cuts through the sweetness of the strawberries and provides a powerful but totally pleasurable contrast in flavors. For a more subtle statement, use half the amount of reduced vinegar. When strawberries are out of season, the balsamic vinegar syrup is great with a vanilla gelato (pages 26–27) or Crème Fraîche Gelato (page 90).

Make the Strawberry Gelato above; just after churning gradually squeeze the balsamic syrup from a squeeze bottle over the top and quickly and lightly swirl in a zigzag pattern with a spoon or butter knife. Alternatively, transfer one third of the gelato to the container you're freezing it in and squeeze one third of the syrup over it. Repeat layering with the remaining gelato and syrup, then freeze for at least 2 hours before serving.

BALSAMIC VINEGAR SYRUP

MAKES JUST UNDER ½ CUP

Pour 2 cups of balsamic vinegar in a medium saucepan and place over medium heat. Bring to a boil, then reduce the heat to low and simmer until thickened and slightly sticky and reduced to a little less than ½ cup, about 30 minutes. Watch the pan carefully; err on the side of caution and measure the reduction as soon as you think it's just under ½ cup. You don't want it to reduce any further or it can become too sticky and harden. (If this happens, you'll have to discard it; pour boiling water over the vinegar to soften it so it will come off the pan.) Pour into a bowl and stir often for a few minutes; the vinegar will thicken further as it cools. Cool completely, then pour into a squeeze bottle. If not using right away, store in the refrigerator and bring to room temperature before using.

BLACKBERRY GELATO

Like blueberries, blackberries are rich in antioxidants and are nutritional powerhouses. They provide an intense fruity flavor with hints of lemon, and they impart a beautiful soft purple color. Blackberry Gelato and Peach Gelato (opposite) make a delectable pair.

Plain Base (page 22)

3 cups fresh blackberries

1 tablespoon sugar

2 teaspoons fresh lemon juice

Make the Plain Base and chill as directed.

Combine the blackberries, sugar, and lemon juice in a food processor and puree, scraping down the sides of the machine once or twice if needed. Pour through a fine-mesh strainer into a bowl, pressing down on the solids to extract all the liquid. Discard the solids. Cover and refrigerate the puree until cold, about 1 hour.

Gently whisk the blackberry puree into the base. Pour the mixture into the container of an ice cream machine and churn according to the manufacturer's instructions. Transfer to an airtight container and freeze for at least 2 hours before serving.

PEACH GELATO

Use red, pink, white, or yellow peaches, or a combination—whatever's the freshest, juiciest, and most aromatic. Extend the season by stocking your freezer with sliced peaches so you can bring a little summer into the colder months. For a refreshing touch, garnish this gelato with fresh mint leaves.

Plain Base (page 22)

1 pound peaches

1 teaspoon fresh lemon juice

Make the Plain Base and chill as directed.

To blanch the peaches and remove their skins: Prepare a large bowl of ice water. Bring a large saucepan of water to a boil. Using the tip of a paring knife, cut a small X into the bottom of the peaches. Immerse the peaches in the water and leave for about 1 minute to loosen the skins (the riper the peach, the less time required). Using a slotted spoon, remove the peaches, immediately plunge them into the bowl of ice water, and let them sit until cool enough to handle, about 1 minute. Peel the peaches using a paring knife, then remove the pit and roughly chop the flesh.

Combine the peach flesh and lemon juice in a food processor and puree, scraping down the sides of the machine once or twice if needed. Pour through a fine-mesh strainer into a bowl, pressing down on the solids to extract all the liquid. Discard the solids. Cover and refrigerate the puree until cold, about 1 hour.

Gently whisk the peach puree into the base. Pour the mixture into the container of an ice cream machine and churn according to the manufacturer's instructions. Transfer to an airtight container and freeze for at least 2 hours before serving.

BLUEBERRY GELATO

This gelato has a beautiful periwinkle blue color and makes the most of the relatively subtle flavor of the blueberries. If you're lucky enough to find late-summer wild blueberries picked fresh from the bush, this gelato is just the thing for them. Blueberries are high in vitamin C, and if you eat a whole pint—which you just might do—you'll be getting 20 percent of your recommended daily amount of fiber and lots of antioxidants. Photograph on page 65.

Plain Base (page 22)

3 cups fresh blueberries

¼ cup sugar

2 tablespoons fresh lemon juice

Make the Plain Base and chill as directed.

Place the blueberries in a medium saucepan. Sprinkle with the sugar, then add the lemon juice; toss until the sugar is dissolved and the blueberries are well coated. Let sit for 30 minutes, stirring occasionally.

Place the pan of blueberries over medium-low heat and cook until the blueberries pop and soften completely and the syrup just starts to thicken, about 10 minutes. Remove from the heat and let cool to room temperature. Transfer to a container, cover, and refrigerate until cold, at least 2 hours. (The blueberries may be prepared a day ahead.)

Place the blueberries in a blender or food processor, add half of the base, and blend until fully incorporated. Whisk into the remaining base. Pour the mixture into the container of an ice cream machine and churn according to the manufacturer's instructions. Transfer to an airtight container and freeze for at least 2 hours before serving.

KEY LIME WITH GRAHAM CRACKER GELATO

Tangy, tart, and refreshing, with a bit of graham cracker crunch—just like the pie.

One of Ciao Bella's most popular recent flavor creations, this started as a seasonal offering for our chef customers and became wildly successful in our gelaterie. The popularity of Key Lime with Graham Cracker Gelato was a bit of a surprise because its flavor is decidedly tart, while Americans tend to have sweeter palates. There's always a fine line between creating what chefs appreciate and what customers will like, but in this case everyone was happy. This flavor is so popular that in less than a year it became our number-one retail gelato flavor in New York City.

Plain Base (page 22)

3 tablespoons fresh lime juice, preferably Key lime

2 teaspoons grated lime zest

¾ cup crushed graham crackers (see Note), frozen

Make the Plain Base and chill as directed.

Gently whisk the lime juice and zest into the base. Pour the mixture into the container of an ice cream machine and churn according to the manufacturer's instructions. Just after

churning quickly stir in the graham cracker crumbs. Transfer to an airtight container and freeze for at least 2 hours before serving.

NOTE

To crush graham crackers, place about 5 graham crackers in a large zip-top bag. Place on a work surface and roll over them with a rolling pin, heavy jar, or wine bottle. Alternatively, break them up a bit by hand, then process in a food processor into crumbs.

APPLE CARAMEL CRISP GELATO

Tender, sweet apples; melt-in-your-mouth caramel; and flaky, buttery pastry all come together in this upscale rendition of apple pie.

Plain Base (page 22)

2 tablespoons unsalted butter, plus more for greasing

⅓ sheet frozen puff pastry, defrosted

2 large apples, peeled, cored, and cut into ¼-inch-wide wedges

½ cup packed light brown sugar

⅛ teaspoon ground cinnamon

2 teaspoons fresh lemon juice

2 teaspoons rum (light or dark) or whiskey

½ cup Caramel Sauce (page 55), at room temperature

Make the Plain Base and chill as directed.

Preheat the oven to 400°F and butter a baking sheet.

Cut the puff pastry into ½-inch squares and place on the prepared baking sheet. Place in the oven and bake for 15 to 20 minutes, until puffed and golden. Remove from the oven and let cool completely. Place in a container and freeze until ready to use. (The puff pastry may be prepared a day ahead.)

In a medium skillet, melt the butter over medium-high heat. Add the apples and sauté, stirring occasionally, until just beginning to brown, about 5 minutes. Add the brown sugar and cinnamon. Continue to cook, stirring, until the apples are very soft and deep golden, about 5 minutes. Add the lemon juice and rum and cook, stirring, for 1 minute. Remove the skillet from the heat and let cool completely. Transfer to a bowl, cover, and refrigerate until cold, about 1 hour.

Pour the custard into the container of an ice cream machine and churn according to the manufacturer's instructions. Add the caramelized apples 5 minutes before the churning is completed. Just after churning, stir in the puff pastry squares, then gradually squeeze the caramel sauce from a squeeze bottle over the top and quickly and lightly swirl in a zigzag pattern with a spoon or butter knife. Alternatively, transfer one third of the gelato to the container you're freezing it in and squeeze one third of the caramel over it. Repeat layering with the remaining gelato and caramel, then freeze for at least 2 hours before serving.

" **EVERY SUNDAY** my mother found the time to make dessert. She'd look around the house and garden, and like a magician come up with zabaione, Chantilly cream, or fruit salad. But when guests were coming, she'd make her famous apple cake—just incredible. "

—CHEF DANILO

BANANA GELATO

One of Ciao Bella's original flavors, this gelato is absolutely bursting with a pure banana taste, with just a hint of lemon juice for a refreshing touch. Feel free to use overripe bananas, as the riper the bananas the sweeter the gelato. To ripen bananas quickly, store them in a brown paper bag overnight.

Plain Base (page 22)

2 ripe bananas, chilled

1 tablespoon sugar

½ tablespoon fresh lemon juice

Make the Plain Base and chill as directed.

Place the bananas, sugar, and lemon juice in a blender and add half the base. Blend until smooth, then whisk into the remaining base. Pour the mixture into the container of an ice cream machine and churn according to the manufacturer's instructions. Transfer to an airtight container and freeze for at least 2 hours before serving.

BANANA WITH WALNUT PRALINE GELATO

Make the Banana Gelato above; just after churning add 1 cup Walnut Praline pieces (at right). Transfer to an airtight container and freeze for at least 2 hours before serving.

WALNUT PRALINES
MAKES ABOUT 2 DOZEN PRALINES

Inspired by New Orleans pecan pralines, this recipe is instead made with walnuts, another example of Ciao Bella putting our spin on a regional favorite.

1¼ cups granulated sugar

¾ cup light brown sugar

½ cup evaporated milk

4 tablespoons (½ stick) unsalted butter, chilled and cut into pieces

1 teaspoon pure vanilla extract

1½ cups chopped walnuts

Line a rimmed baking sheet with wax paper or a silicone mat. In a medium heavy-bottom saucepan, combine the sugars and milk. Place over medium heat and bring to a simmer without stirring. Lower the heat and cook, stirring, until a candy thermometer registers 235 to 245°F. Test by dropping a small spoonful into a glass of very cold water; using your fingers, you'll be able to form the syrup into a soft ball that will flatten when removed from the water.

Remove the mixture from the heat and add the butter, vanilla, and walnuts and stir for about 1 minute, until the mixture is no longer shiny. Immediately drop the mixture by tablespoons onto the baking sheet. Set aside and let cool completely, then remove from the sheet and store in an airtight container.

MAPLE WALNUT GELATO

This gelato is light and airy and extra-sweet, which makes it particularly hard to put down. We've noticed that this flavor has become increasingly hard to find commercially—all the more reason to make it at home and keep the New England tradition alive. The sweetness of the maple syrup definitely asserts itself; feel free to reduce the amount of sugar if you like, but keep the full amount of maple syrup to get the complete effect. Use lighter grade A maple syrup for a more delicate flavor and grade B for a darker, deeper maple taste.

Plain Base (page 22)

6 tablespoons pure maple syrup, chilled

1 cup coarsely chopped roasted walnuts (see page 47), frozen

Make the Plain Base and chill as directed.

Gently whisk the maple syrup into the base. Pour the mixture into the container of an ice cream machine and churn according to the manufacturer's instructions. Add the chopped walnuts 5 minutes before the churning is completed. Transfer to an airtight container and freeze for at least 2 hours before serving.

PUMPKIN AND SPICE GELATO

Nothing captures the season as well as this flavor; it tastes just like a slice of pumpkin pie without the crust. The beautiful autumn-orange color and warming spices make it the perfect fall comfort food and a standout at a holiday dinner.

Plain Base (page 22)

1 cup pure pumpkin puree (not pumpkin pie mix), chilled

¼ cup sugar

¼ teaspoon pure vanilla extract

½ teaspoon ground cinnamon

Pinch of ground cloves

Make the Plain Base and chill as directed.

Place the pumpkin, sugar, vanilla, cinnamon, and cloves in a blender and add half of the base. Blend until smooth, then whisk into the remaining base. Pour the mixture into the container of an ice cream machine and churn according to the manufacturer's instructions. Transfer to an airtight container and freeze for at least 2 hours before serving.

BUTTER PECAN GELATO

A Southern favorite and one of the most popular flavors in the United States, this gelato has a comforting down-home familiarity.

½ cup (1 stick) unsalted butter

2 cups whole milk

1 cup heavy cream

⅔ cup sugar

4 large egg yolks

¼ teaspoon pure vanilla extract

1 cup roasted pecan halves (see page 47), frozen

Place the butter in a small saucepan over medium heat. Heat the butter, stirring often, until it melts completely and just turns a light golden brown color, about 5 minutes. Watch carefully, as even a few seconds too long can cause the butter to burn. Remove from the heat, pour into a medium heat-proof bowl, and let cool slightly.

In a heavy-bottom saucepan, combine the milk and cream. Place over medium-low heat and cook, stirring occasionally so a skin doesn't form, until tiny bubbles start to form around the edges and the mixture reaches a temperature of 170°F.

Meanwhile, whisk the sugar with the butter until smooth, then whisk in the egg yolks until well incorporated and the mixture is thick. Temper the egg yolks by very slowly pouring in the hot milk mixture while whisking continuously. Return the custard to the saucepan and place over low heat. Heat, stirring frequently with a wooden spoon, until the custard is thick enough to coat the back of the spoon and it reaches a temperature of 185°F. Do not bring to a boil.

Pour the custard through a fine-mesh strainer into a clean bowl and let cool completely, stirring often. To cool the custard quickly, make an ice bath by filling a large bowl with ice and water and placing the bowl with the custard in it; stir the custard until cooled. Once completely cooled, cover and refrigerate until very cold, at least 4 hours or overnight.

Gently whisk the vanilla into the custard. Pour it into the container of an ice cream machine and churn according to the manufacturer's instructions. Add the pecans 5 minutes before the churning is completed. Transfer to an airtight container and freeze for at least 2 hours before serving.

Fun Flavors for Kids

—The gelati on the following pages are a fantasy come true for any child, and adults will appreciate their playfulness, nostalgia, and familiarity. Seek out all-natural candies and cookies, as Ciao Bella does, to make your indulgence a pure one.

HAZELNUT BISCOTTI GELATO

This was Ciao Bella's first award-winning flavor—a unique take on the ever-popular Cookies and Cream and a sweet and extra-nutty variation on the classic creamy Hazelnut Gelato (page 39). Use your favorite brand of biscotti for this recipe.

Plain Base (page 22)

½ cup roasted hazelnuts (see page 47), cooled and ground to a paste in a coffee grinder

1 cup chopped almond biscotti, frozen

Make the Plain Base and chill as directed.

In a blender, combine the hazelnut paste with half of the base and blend until fully incorporated. Whisk into the remaining base, pour into the container of an ice cream machine, and churn according to the manufacturer's instructions. Just after churning, quickly stir in the chopped biscotti. Transfer to an airtight container and freeze for at least 2 hours before serving.

COOKIES AND CREAM GELATO

Large pieces of cookies and a generous amount of crumbs make this classic chocolate cookie gelato a real treat. It is one of the top flavors with kids at our gelaterie.

Plain Base (page 22)

2 chocolate sandwich cookies, finely chopped and frozen

3 chocolate sandwich cookies, coarsely chopped (leave some bigger pieces if you like) and frozen

Make the Plain Base and chill as directed.

Gently stir the finely chopped chocolate sandwich cookies into the base. Pour the mixture into the container of an ice cream machine and churn according to the manufacturer's instructions. Add the coarsely chopped chocolate sandwich cookies 5 minutes before the churning is completed. Transfer to an airtight container and freeze for at least 2 hours before serving.

CHOCOLATE S'MORES GELATO

Crunchy graham crackers, chewy marshmallows, and rich chocolate come together in this reinterpretation of a campfire treat, another example of the particularly American combination of creativity and tradition.

2 cups whole milk

1 cup heavy cream

¼ cup unsweetened cocoa powder

4 ounces milk chocolate, finely chopped

4 egg yolks

½ cup granulated sugar

¼ cup finely chopped graham crackers (leave some bigger pieces if you like), chilled

½ cup mini marshmallows, chilled

In a heavy-bottom saucepan, combine the milk and cream. Place over medium-low heat and cook, stirring occasionally so a skin doesn't form, until tiny bubbles start to form around the edges and the mixture reaches a temperature of 170°F. Turn off the heat and whisk in the cocoa powder. Add the chopped chocolate and stir or whisk until the chocolate is completely melted and the mixture is smooth.

Meanwhile, in a medium heat-proof bowl, whisk the egg yolks until smooth. Gradually whisk in the sugar until it is well incorporated and the mixture is thick and pale yellow. Temper the egg yolks by very slowly pouring in the hot milk mixture while whisking continuously. Return the custard to the saucepan and place over low heat. Cook, stirring frequently with a wooden spoon, until the custard is thick enough to coat the back of the spoon and it reaches a temperature of 185°F. Do not bring to a boil.

Pour the custard through a fine-mesh strainer into a clean bowl and cool completely, stirring often. To cool the custard quickly, make an ice bath by filling a large bowl with ice and water and placing the bowl with the custard in it; stir until cooled. Once completely cooled, cover and refrigerate until very cold, at least 4 hours or overnight.

Remove the custard from the refrigerator and gently stir in the chopped graham crackers. Pour the mixture into the container of an ice cream machine and churn according to the manufacturer's instructions. Add the mini marshmallows 5 minutes before the churning is completed. Transfer to an airtight container and freeze for at least 2 hours before serving.

CINNAMON WITH OATMEAL COOKIE GELATO

Fans of Ciao Bella's Oatmeal Cookie Gelato, made with Eleni's Oatmeal Cookies, will love to re-create it at home. Her recipe is specially modified here for inclusion in ice cream.

Plain Base (page 22)

¼ teaspoon pure vanilla extract

2 teaspoons ground cinnamon

1 cup crumbled oatmeal cookies, frozen

Make the Plain Base and chill as directed.

Gently whisk the vanilla and cinnamon into the base. Pour the mixture into the container of an ice cream machine and churn according to the manufacturer's instructions. Add the crumbled oatmeal cookies 5 minutes before the churning is completed. Transfer to an airtight container and freeze for at least 2 hours before serving.

ELENI'S OATMEAL RAISIN COOKIES

MAKES ABOUT 30 COOKIES

1 cup all-purpose flour

½ teaspoon baking powder

½ teaspoon baking soda

¼ teaspoon salt

¼ teaspoon ground cinnamon

10 tablespoons (1¼ sticks) unsalted butter, at
  room temperature

1 cup packed dark brown sugar

¼ cup granulated sugar

1 large egg, at room temperature

½ teaspoon pure vanilla extract

1½ cups whole rolled oats

½ cup raisins

Preheat the oven to 350°F. Line 2 baking sheets with parchment paper and set aside.

In a large bowl, sift together the flour, baking powder, baking soda, salt, and cinnamon, and stir to combine. Set aside.

In the bowl of a stand mixer fitted with the paddle attachment, cream the butter with the sugars until light and fluffy. Add the egg and beat well to incorporate. Add the vanilla and mix until smooth. Add the flour mixture and mix on low speed until smooth. Add the oats and raisins. Mix just until incorporated.

Drop the batter by tablespoons 2 inches apart on the baking sheets. Bake for 15 minutes, or until golden and slightly firm. Transfer to a wire rack, and let cool completely. Cool the baking sheets and continue to make batches of cookies until the dough is used up.

MALTED MILK BALL GELATO

This magical flavor was originally developed for the opening of the Paramount Hotel in New York City. This was the first flavor that marketing director Deborah Holt fell in love with; she talked about it all the time and ate it whenever she could. Despite its popularity, we didn't introduce it into retail until recently; early sales indicate that it might become one of our most popular flavors ever. You can find malted milk powder near the dry milk products in your supermarket, or order it online (see Sources, page 174).

Plain Base (page 22)

¼ cup malt powder

⅛ teaspoon pure vanilla extract

½ cup chopped malted milk balls or mini malted milk balls, frozen

Make the Plain Base and chill as directed.

Gently whisk the malt powder and vanilla into the base. Pour the mixture into the container of an ice cream machine and churn according to the manufacturer's instructions. Add the malted milk balls 5 minutes before the churning is completed. Transfer to an airtight container and freeze for at least 2 hours before serving.

MAPLE GINGERSNAP GELATO

Spicy bits of crunchy-chewy gingersnaps are showcased here in a maple syrup base. Pure enjoyment.

Plain Base (page 22)

6 tablespoons pure maple syrup, chilled

1 cup finely chopped gingersnaps, frozen

Make the Plain Base and chill as directed.

Gently whisk the maple syrup into the base. Pour the mixture into the container of an ice cream machine and churn according to the manufacturer's instructions. Add the chopped gingersnaps 5 minutes before the churning is completed. Transfer to an airtight container and freeze for at least 2 hours before serving.

PEANUT BUTTER GELATO

Both kids and adults come back to the flavor of peanut butter time and again. Ciao Bella once had a peanut butter–chocolate flavor, though it was banned from our factories after a fateful skiing trip where I polished off a whole quart in one sitting. We've included it as a variation below; make it at your own risk. —FW

Plain Base (page 22)

½ cup sweetened smooth peanut butter

Make the Plain Base and chill as directed.

Place the peanut butter in a blender and add half of the base. Blend until smooth, then whisk into the remaining base. Pour the mixture into the container of an ice cream machine and churn according to the manufacturer's instructions. Transfer to an airtight container and freeze for at least 2 hours before serving.

CHOCOLATE PEANUT BUTTER GELATO

Make the Peanut Butter Gelato above, substituting the Chocolate Base (page 25) for the Plain Base.

PEANUT BUTTER WITH STRAWBERRY SWIRL GELATO

A lunchbox favorite reborn in gelato form.

Make the Peanut Butter Gelato above; just after churning, spoon ½ cup strawberry jam (or one of your kids' favorite flavors) over the top and quickly and lightly swirl in a zigzag pattern with a spoon or butter knife. (You may need to thin the jam with a little water to make it easier to swirl.) Alternatively, transfer one third of the gelato to the container you're freezing it in and spoon one third of the jam over it. Repeat layering with the remaining gelato and jam, then freeze for at least 2 hours before serving.

PEPPERMINT STICK GELATO

Flecks of icy peppermint swirled into gelato provide a sweet, chilly blast with every spoonful. It's perfect hot fudge sundae material. For a strong mint effect, you can increase the amount of peppermint extract to ¾ teaspoon. This gelato is my Christmas present to friends and family every year. One year I sent a different flavor and there was a serious rebellion. —FW

Plain Base (page 22)

½ teaspoon peppermint extract

⅔ cup crushed candy canes or peppermint candies (see Note), frozen

Make the Plain Base and chill as directed.

Gently whisk the peppermint extract into the base. Pour the mixture into the container of an ice cream machine and churn according to the manufacturer's instructions. Add the crushed candy halfway through churning. Transfer to an airtight container and freeze for at least 2 hours before serving.

NOTE
To crush candy canes, break them into pieces and pulse in a food processor, or hit them with a food mallet while still in their packages.

MINT CHOCOLATE CHIP GELATO

Cool and clean-tasting, Mint Gelato is delicious flecked with bittersweet chocolate. Using high-quality chocolate instead of the usual chips raises the sophistication of this gelato, and your kids will still love it. As with Peppermint Stick Gelato, for a strong mint effect, you can increase the amount of peppermint extract to ¾ teaspoon.

Plain Base (page 22)

½ teaspoon peppermint extract

¼ cup finely chopped bittersweet chocolate, frozen

Make the Plain Base and chill as directed.

Gently whisk the peppermint extract into the base. Pour the mixture into the container of an ice cream machine and churn according to the manufacturer's instructions. Add the chopped chocolate 5 minutes before the churning is completed. Transfer to an airtight container and freeze for at least 2 hours before serving.

A Note on Mix-ins and Toppings

Traditional Italian gelato—even pistachio—is smooth, but we Americans like stuff in our ice cream. Even the simplest ice cream flavors such as maple walnut, butter pecan, and strawberry traditionally have small bits of fruit and nuts, which add a textural variation to their European forebears. Ben & Jerry's started this modern craze by adding huge chunks of candy to its product, and Steve's Ice Cream, a Boston chain, took it one step further by allowing people to mix in their own ingredients. Thus began a new era, in which ice cream became all about digging for the candy. Though Steve's is now gone, Cold Stone Creamery, MaggieMoo's, and Marble Slab have followed in its footsteps.

At Ciao Bella, we leave the flavor creation in Chef Danilo's hands. He's a purist, but because Ciao Bella is a combination of classic Italian and American, we've made some of our flavors smooth and some not. In our gelaterie we offer a number of toppings; first in popularity is sprinkles, with gummy bears coming in second (though Chef Danilo vows he'll never make a gummy bear gelato). We encourage you to experiment with mix-ins; there is no hard and fast rule other than to limit them to 1 cup per quart so you can still taste your gelato. Look to your favorite foods for inspiration. Lead with your imagination and be creative! —FW

CARAMEL ENGLISH TOFFEE CRUNCH GELATO

Here our inspiration came from the popular American ice cream flavor Heath Bar Crunch, but our version calls for a caramel base plus the candy for a double dose of caramel.

Plain Base (page 22)

¼ cup Caramel Sauce (page 55), at room temperature

½ cup chopped English toffee candy, frozen

Make the Plain Base and chill as directed.

Gently whisk the caramel sauce into the base. Pour the mixture into the container of an ice cream machine and churn according to the manufacturer's instructions. Add the chopped English toffee 5 minutes before the churning is completed. Transfer to an airtight container and freeze for at least 2 hours before serving.

COCONUT-ALMOND GELATO

Reminiscent of an Almond Joy but made with all-natural ingredients.

Plain Base (page 22)

¼ teaspoon almond extract

½ cup shredded sweetened coconut flakes, chilled

¼ cup roasted almonds (see page 47), frozen

2 ounces coarsely chopped bittersweet chocolate, frozen

Make the Plain Base and chill as directed.

Gently whisk the almond extract into the base, then stir in the coconut. Pour the mixture into the container of an ice cream machine and churn according to the manufacturer's instructions. Add the almonds and chocolate 5 minutes before the churning is completed. Transfer to an airtight container and freeze for at least 2 hours before serving.

UNIQUELY
CIAO BELLA

From the beginning Ciao Bella has been best known for its innovative flavors and superior ingredients. Many of our most interesting customers have been chefs, who are always pushing the envelope and testing new territory. You'll find a range of sophisticated yet accessible ingredients in the recipes in this section.

Early in Ciao Bella's history—more than twenty years ago—we developed the Green Tea Gelato for a Japanese restaurant in Manhattan. It was the first non-American, non-Italian flavor, and the other Asian and global flavors included in this section stemmed from its success.

The section concludes with several alcohol-based flavors for adults. Their signature ingredients pack a delightful punch and are a heady finish to any meal.

CRÈME FRAÎCHE GELATO

Chefs appreciate both the subtlety and complexity of crème fraîche. French for "fresh cream," it is a milder and thicker version of sour cream, often used to finish sauces in French cooking. It complements rather than overshadows other flavors, which also makes it a fantastic companion to fruit and fruit-based desserts.

We've provided instructions for making your own crème fraîche, which requires leaving it to thicken overnight at room temperature. Don't worry about the cream going bad—Regan Daley, in her book *In the Sweet Kitchen,* tells us that "the benign live bacteria in the buttermilk will multiply and protect the cream from any harmful bacteria." Prepared crème fraîche, which can be found in the cheese section at gourmet food shops, can be substituted; use 1¾ cups. The yield for this gelato will be a little more than 1 quart.

1½ cups heavy cream

¼ cup buttermilk

Plain Base (page 22)

To make the crème fraîche: In a bowl or container, stir together the cream and buttermilk. Cover loosely and set aside at room temperature overnight, or until thickened to the consistency of thick cream, slightly thinner than sour cream. Stir the mixture, then cover loosely again and refrigerate until cold, at least 2 hours or up till overnight.

Meanwhile, make the Plain Base and chill as directed.

Combine the crème fraîche mixture with the base. Pour the mixture into the container of an ice cream machine and churn according to the manufacturer's instructions. Transfer to an airtight container and freeze for at least 2 hours before serving.

BANANA CAJETA CASHEW GELATO

Cajeta is a goat's-milk caramel popular in Mexico where it's made into candies or drizzled over ice cream and other desserts. The word *cajeta* is Spanish for "small box," named for the containers the caramel was traditionally packed in.

Making your own cajeta is worth the extra bit of work, but you can also buy it (see Sources, page 174) or substitute its South American cousin, dulce de leche (see page 105).

Plain Base (page 22)

2 ripe bananas, chilled

1 tablespoon sugar

½ tablespoon fresh lemon juice

½ cup coarsely chopped roasted salted cashews (see page 47), frozen

½ cup cajeta (at right), slightly warmed

Make the Plain Base and chill as directed.

Place the bananas, sugar, and lemon juice in a blender and add half of the base. Blend until smooth, then whisk into the remaining base. Pour the mixture into the container of an ice cream machine and churn according to the manufacturer's instructions. Add the cashews 5 minutes before the churning is completed.

Just after churning, drizzle the cajeta over the top and quickly and lightly swirl in a zigzag pattern with a spoon or butter knife.

CAJETA

MAKES ABOUT 3 CUPS

2 cups goat's milk

2 cups sugar

⅛ teaspoon pure vanilla extract, preferably Mexican (see Sources, page 174)

½ teaspoon baking soda dissolved in 1 tablespoon water

In a large, heavy-bottom saucepan, combine the milk, sugar, and vanilla and place over medium heat. Bring to a simmer, stirring constantly with a wooden spoon to dissolve the sugar. Remove the pan from the heat and stir in the dissolved baking soda. When the bubbling stops, return the pan to the heat, bring back to a simmer, and cook, stirring often, for 1 hour, or until the mixture starts to thicken and turn golden. At this point the cajeta will start to thicken fast, so don't leave the pan unattended. Continue to cook, stirring constantly so it doesn't burn or stick to the bottom of the pan, for another 20 minutes, or until the cajeta is a rich brown color and thick enough to coat the back of the spoon. It should cool to a medium-thick caramel consistency. If it's too thick, add a small amount of water; if it's too thin, continue to cook until thickened.

Transfer to a container, let cool, then cover and refrigerate until ready to use. Warm slightly before serving. It will keep for about 1 month in the refrigerator.

ROSEMARY AND OLIVE OIL GELATO

This savory gelato—one of our more unusual flavors—was inspired by trends in olive oil ice creams that we saw on the innovative New York City restaurant scene. Ciao Bella's take was to add rosemary, which has a slightly bitter, woody taste that complements a wide variety of foods. The rosemary is infused in milk for forty-eight hours, so be sure to allot time for that step.

½ cup coarsely chopped fresh rosemary

2 cups whole milk

1 cup heavy cream

4 large egg yolks

⅔ cup sugar

1 teaspoon extra-virgin olive oil

In a medium bowl or container, combine the rosemary and milk. Cover and refrigerate for 48 hours, stirring the mixture after 24 hours and again just before straining.

Strain the rosemary-infused milk into a large heavy-bottom saucepan, pressing on the solids to extract all the flavored milk mixture. Discard the rosemary and add the cream. Place over medium-low heat and cook, stirring occasionally so a skin doesn't form, until tiny bubbles start to form around the edges and the mixture reaches a temperature of 170°F.

Meanwhile, in a medium heat-proof bowl, whisk the egg yolks until smooth. Gradually whisk in the sugar until it is well incorporated and the mixture is thick and pale yellow. Temper the egg yolks by very slowly pouring in the hot milk mixture while whisking continuously. Return the custard to the saucepan and place over low heat. Cook, stirring frequently with a wooden spoon, until the custard is thick enough to coat the back of the spoon and it reaches a temperature of 185°F. Do not bring to a boil.

Pour the custard through a fine-mesh strainer into a clean bowl and cool completely, stirring every 5 minutes or so. To cool the custard quickly, make an ice bath by filling a large bowl with ice and water and placing the bowl with the custard in it; stir the custard until cooled. Once completely cooled, cover and refrigerate until very cold, at least 4 hours or overnight.

Remove the custard from the refrigerator and whisk in the olive oil. Pour the mixture into the container of an ice cream machine and churn according to the manufacturer's instructions. Transfer to an airtight container and freeze for at least 2 hours before serving.

Flavors We May Never See at Ciao Bella

- Huitlacoche (Corn Smut) Gelato—Developed for a special James Beard House dinner. It was the worst flavor we ever made; it might have been that there was too much cognac, but I still blame the fungus.

- Mango Peppercorn Sorbetto—Not complex enough.

- Pear and Gorgonzola Sorbetto—Ciao Bella actually produced this one but it did not sell well; those of us at the company loved it at first, but the cheese continued to ripen in the container and the result was not pretty.

- Juniper Gelato—I really like the resin and smoky smell of juniper; I'll convince the rest of the crew someday.

- Lemon Basil—I loved this one, but it didn't make the cut—that's just how it is sometimes.

- Mustard Gelato—You really need to love mustard to appreciate it, and in the end only our mustard-fanatic marketing director Deborah Holt and I could stand it.

- Jasmine Almond Milk Sorbetto—A little too unusual.

- Pesca Deliziosa Gelato—A traditional dessert from Piedmont containing chocolate, peaches, and Amaretti cookies. Not a winner . . . yet.

- White Truffle Gelato—There was a big debate between purists who refused to put truffles in their gelato and truffle lovers who wanted truffles in everything.

- Green Tomato Sorbetto—Interesting but a little extreme.

- Persimmon Sorbetto—Too expensive.

- Raw Fish Sorbetto—Requested by a sushi restaurant, but I refused to make it—for obvious reasons.

—DZ

LEMON GELATO

My wife, Alice, loved this flavor so much when I created it that we served this tangy, refreshing gelato at our wedding in 1991. The caterer thought it was vanilla because of its pale, almost white color—but if any gelato is a stand-alone flavor, it's this one, so imagine my surprise when I saw they had set up a sundae bar around it! Lemon Gelato is one of the flavors selected for the Ottimo sandwiches (see page 168). —FW

Plain Base (page 22)

¼ cup fresh lemon juice

2 teaspoons grated lemon zest

Make the Plain Base and chill as directed.

Gently whisk the lemon juice and zest into the base. Pour the mixture into the container of an ice cream machine and churn according to the manufacturer's instructions. Transfer to an airtight container and freeze for at least 2 hours before serving.

LEMON POPPY SEED GELATO
Make the Lemon Gelato above. Add 1 tablespoon poppy seeds 5 minutes before the churning is completed, then transfer to an airtight container and freeze for at least 2 hours before serving.

ROSE PETAL GELATO

This striking pink gelato is perfect for Mother's Day or any romantic occasion: Why not buy a heart-shaped mold and surprise your sweetheart with a heart-shaped gelato cake (see page 162) for Valentine's Day or your anniversary? The rosewater gives a delicate floral flavor and aroma, and the beet juice provides an all-natural pink coloring; no artificial food dyes are needed. Candied rose petals add an exotic and very sweet touch, but the gelato is equally lovely without them. Photograph opposite, bottom.

This is the favorite flavor of our editor, Aliza Fogelson. As she explains: "When I lived in France, I loved eating rose- and violet-flavored desserts. Floral flavors are popular there (whereas a lot of people here think they taste like perfume!). The combination of rose flavor and gelato is irresistible to me, partly because I enjoy each of those two things individually and partly because eating it reminds me of a place I adore—Paris."

Plain Base (page 22)

1 tablespoon rosewater (see Sources, page 174)

1 teaspoon beet juice (see Note)

¼ cup candied rose petals (see Sources, page 174), optional

Make the Plain Base and chill as directed.

Gently whisk the rosewater and beet juice into the base. Pour the mixture into the container of an ice cream machine and churn according to the manufacturer's instructions. Add the candied rose petals, if using, 5 minutes before the churning is completed. Transfer to an airtight container and freeze for at least 2 hours before serving.

NOTE
To make a small amount of beet juice, peel a beet, finely grate a small amount, then simply squeeze the beet pulp with your fingers to extract the juice. To keep your fingers from turning red, wear plastic gloves or simply place a plastic bag over your hand while squeezing.

FRESH MINT GELATO

Fresh Mint Gelato is one of the last flavors I developed before Chef Danilo took over the flavor creation role. It is now a signature Ciao Bella flavor. It was inspired by my favorite summertime drink, the southside—a variation of the mojito.

The mint is infused in milk for forty-eight hours to slowly bring out its flavor, so be sure to plan in advance. Photograph on page 91. —FW

½ cup coarsely chopped fresh mint

2 cups whole milk

1 cup heavy cream

4 large egg yolks

⅔ cup sugar

In a medium bowl or container, combine the mint and milk. Cover and refrigerate for 48 hours, stirring the mixture after 24 hours and just before heating.

Remove the milk from the refrigerator and pour it into a heavy-bottom saucepan. Add the cream. Place over medium-low heat and cook, stirring occasionally so a skin doesn't form, until tiny bubbles start to form around the edges and the mixture reaches a temperature of 170°F. Remove the pan from the heat and set aside for 20 minutes. Strain the mixture into a heat-proof bowl, pressing on the mint to extract all the flavored milk. (Discard the mint.)

Return the milk to the saucepan and bring the liquid back to 170°F.

Meanwhile, in a medium heat-proof bowl, whisk the egg yolks until smooth. Gradually whisk in the sugar until it is well incorporated and the mixture is thick and pale yellow. Temper the egg yolks by very slowly pouring in the hot milk mixture while whisking continuously. Return the custard to the saucepan and place over low heat. Cook, stirring frequently with a wooden spoon, until the custard is thick enough to coat the back of the spoon and it reaches a temperature of 185°F. Do not bring to a boil.

Pour the custard through a fine-mesh strainer into a clean bowl. Cool completely, stirring every 5 minutes or so. To cool the custard quickly, make an ice bath by filling a large bowl with ice and water and placing the bowl with the custard in it; stir the custard until cooled. Once completely cooled, cover and refrigerate until very cold, at least 4 hours or overnight.

Pour the mixture into the container of an ice cream machine and churn according to the manufacturer's instructions. Transfer to an airtight container and freeze for at least 2 hours before serving.

Global Inspirations

—Ciao Bella has developed a decidedly global feel since Chef Danilo came on board. Chef Danilo has lived all over the world, speaks four languages, and ran a restaurant in the Caribbean. Travel is his inspiration. He embraces the essence of a place—the aromas, colors, textures—and translates it into the flavors that have made Ciao Bella what it is today. Ciao Bella's diverse workforce—many staff members hailing from Latin America and the Caribbean—has also contributed to the development of some of our international flavors.

We encourage you to celebrate your heritage, the places you've visited, and your favorite types of cuisine as you continue to experiment with gelato at home. —FW

RED BEAN GELATO

The red beans in this recipe are adzuki beans, which are commonly cooked with sugar into a paste and used in a wide variety of Chinese and Japanese sweets. Adzukis are also prized in macrobiotic cooking for their easy digestibility and high fiber, protein, and mineral content. They make a deliciously subtle, nutty-tasting gelato. Photograph below.

Plain Base (page 22)

One 15-ounce can adzuki beans, rinsed and
   drained

¼ cup sugar

⅛ teaspoon pure vanilla extract

Make the Plain Base and chill as directed.

Combine the adzuki beans and sugar in a small saucepan, place over medium-low heat, and cook, stirring constantly, until the sugar is absorbed and the beans are very soft, 10 to 15 minutes. Transfer to a bowl, let cool, then cover and refrigerate until cold, about 2 hours. The beans can be prepared a day in advance.

Place the adzuki beans and vanilla in a blender and add half of the base. Blend until smooth, strain, then whisk the liquid into the remaining base. Pour the mixture into the container of an ice cream machine and churn according to the manufacturer's instructions. Transfer to an airtight container and freeze for at least 2 hours before serving.

BLACK SESAME GELATO

This Asian favorite has a slightly smoky, nutty flavor and a pleasant crunch. Although tan sesame seeds are favored in Western cooking, the black variety is appreciated in Asia for its stronger, slightly bitter flavor, and black sesame seeds make a dramatic garnish. You can find them in Asian markets.

Plain Base (page 22)

¾ cup black sesame seeds

⅛ teaspoon pure vanilla extract

Make the Plain Base and chill as directed.

Place half of the base in a blender and add ½ cup of the sesame seeds and the vanilla. Blend until incorporated, then whisk into the remaining base. Pour the mixture into the container of an ice cream machine and churn according to the manufacturer's instructions. Add the remaining ¼ cup sesame seeds 5 minutes before the churning is completed. Transfer to an airtight container and freeze for at least 2 hours before serving.

GINGER GELATO

This bold, pungent flavor was originally intended as an offering to round out Ciao Bella's Asian selections, but it has also become very popular in American and French restaurants as an accompaniment to pear, apple, and nut tarts. The ginger may curdle the milk and cream mixture, but it won't affect the end result.

2 cups whole milk

1 cup heavy cream

One 2-inch piece of ginger, peeled and grated (2 tablespoons)

Pinch of salt

4 egg yolks

¾ cup sugar

In a heavy-bottom saucepan, combine the milk, cream, ginger, and salt. Place over medium-low heat and cook, stirring occasionally so a skin doesn't form, until tiny bubbles start to form around the edges and the mixture reaches a temperature of 170°F. Remove from the heat and set aside for 1 hour, then strain the mixture into a bowl, pressing on the ginger to extract all the liquid. Return the custard to the pan and reheat to 170°F.

Meanwhile, in a medium heat-proof bowl, whisk the egg yolks until smooth. Gradually whisk in the sugar until it is well incorporated and the mixture is thick and pale yellow. Temper the egg yolks by very slowly pouring in the hot milk mixture while whisking continuously. Return the custard to the saucepan and place over low heat. Cook, stirring frequently with a wooden spoon, until the custard is thick enough to coat the back of the spoon and it reaches a temperature of 185°F. Do not bring to a boil.

Pour the custard through a fine-mesh strainer into a clean bowl and cool completely, stirring every 5 minutes or so. To cool the custard quickly, make an ice bath by filling a large bowl with ice and water and placing the bowl with the custard in it; stir until cooled. Once completely cooled, cover and refrigerate until very cold, at least 4 hours or overnight.

Pour the custard into the container of an ice cream machine and churn according to the manufacturer's instructions. Transfer to an airtight container and freeze for at least 2 hours before serving.

GREEN TEA GELATO

This was our first globally inspired flavor, developed in partnership with Hatsuhana restaurant in New York. Ciao Bella was selling lemon sorbetto to the chefs, and they asked if we would make a green tea flavor. They introduced us to matcha gunpowder tea, made from powdered whole tea leaves (since the leaves themselves are consumed, this tea is particularly high in antioxidants). Matcha works well in food preparations, especially gelato, and is prized for its striking green color; simply blend it with the base— no brewing required—and the custard is ready to be churned. If you like a stronger brew, you can add an extra tablespoon of tea to the base. Matcha tea is available at Japanese markets and online (see Sources, page 174).

Plain Base (page 22)

1 tablespoon matcha gunpowder tea

Make the Plain Base and chill as directed.

Place half of the base in a blender and add the tea. Blend until smooth, then whisk into the remaining base. Pour the mixture into the container of an ice cream machine and churn according to the manufacturer's instructions. Transfer to an airtight container and freeze for at least 2 hours before serving.

MEXICAN CHOCOLATE GELATO

Chocolate, the food of the gods according to the Maya and Aztecs, played a part in their religion and ritual and it was combined with honey, seeds, and spices in a variety of drinks. This gelato is reminiscent of Mexican drinking chocolate, which is made from dark bitter chocolate, sugar, cinnamon, and sometimes nuts.

Chocolate Base (page 25)

⅛ teaspoon ground cinnamon

½ cup chopped toasted almonds
   (see page 47), frozen

Make the Chocolate Base and chill as directed.

Gently whisk the cinnamon into the base. Pour the mixture into the container of an ice cream machine and churn according to the manufacturer's instructions. Add the almonds 5 minutes before the churning is completed. Transfer to an airtight container and freeze for at least 2 hours before serving.

“**TRAVEL AND MEETING PEOPLE** from other countries is the best way to open up your mind. The different cultures, colors, smells, and emotions translate into recipes. I love simplicity and innovation, and they influence my gelato creations.”

—CHEF DANILO

MEXICAN COFFEE GELATO

This one takes its cue from another Mexican-style hot beverage, a traditional sweet coffee with strong notes of cinnamon and orange. Photograph on page 11.

Plain Base (page 22), substituting dark brown sugar for the granulated sugar

1 tablespoon instant coffee granules

1 tablespoon unsweetened cocoa powder

¾ teaspoon pure vanilla extract

⅛ teaspoon ground cinnamon

1 teaspoon grated orange zest

Make the Plain Base and chill as directed.

Place half of the base in a blender and add the coffee, cocoa powder, vanilla, and cinnamon. Blend until smooth, then whisk into the remaining base and stir in the orange zest. Pour the mixture into the container of an ice cream machine and churn according to the manufacturer's instructions. Transfer to an airtight container and freeze for at least 2 hours before serving.

DULCE DE LECHE GELATO

Latin American flavors are quickly entering the mainstream, and top on the list is the alluringly sweet dulce de leche, a South American–style caramel that has made its way into countless dessert preparations. We've included a recipe for making your own dulce de leche here; you can also buy it premade (see Sources, page 174).

Plain Base (page 22)

1 cup Dulce de Leche (at right)

Make the Plain Base and chill as directed.

Place half of the base in a blender and add ½ cup of the dulce de leche. Blend until smooth, then whisk into the remaining base. Pour the mixture into the container of an ice cream machine and churn according to the manufacturer's instructions.

In a small saucepan over low heat, gently warm the remaining ½ cup dulce de leche. Just after churning the custard, drizzle the dulce de leche over the top and quickly and lightly swirl in a zigzag pattern with a spoon or butter knife. Alternatively, transfer one third of the gelato to the container you're freezing it in and drizzle one third of the dulce de leche over it. Repeat layering with the remaining gelato and dulce de leche, then freeze for at least 2 hours before serving.

DULCE DE LECHE
MAKES 1 CUP

All that is involved in this easy but somewhat unusual technique is simmering an unopened can of sweetened condensed milk for 2 hours.

One 14-ounce can sweetened condensed milk

Fill a large saucepan with water. Remove the label from the can and place the can in the water. Bring to a boil, then reduce the heat to medium-low and simmer for 2 hours, making sure the can is covered with water at all times. Remove the can using tongs and transfer to a wire rack to cool completely (this can take up to 1 hour). Open the can, spoon the dulce de leche into a container, cover, and refrigerate until ready to use.

SAFFRON SPICE GELATO

Throughout the years Ciao Bella has donated thousands of gallons of gelato to a vast array of worthy charities. Saffron Spice Gelato—warming and a little exotic—was first developed for a Moroccan-themed charity benefit for the Urban Stages Theater in New York, a company that produces exceptional new works by artists of diverse cultural backgrounds.

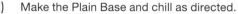

Plain Base (page 22)

¼ cup whole milk

½ teaspoon saffron threads

¼ cup honey

⅛ teaspoon almond extract

⅛ teaspoon ground cinnamon

⅛ teaspoon ground cardamom

⅛ teaspoon ground ginger

Pinch of freshly ground black pepper

½ cup roasted pistachios (see page 47), frozen

Make the Plain Base and chill as directed.

In a small saucepan, warm the milk over medium-low heat just until small bubbles start to form around the edges. Remove the pan from the heat, crumble in the saffron, and set aside to infuse for 20 minutes. Pour the milk through a fine-mesh strainer into a bowl, pressing on the solids to extract all the liquid. Discard the saffron. Refrigerate until cold, about 30 minutes.

In a blender, combine half of the base with the saffron-infused milk, honey, almond extract, cinnamon, cardamom, ginger, and black pepper and blend until smooth. Whisk into the remaining base, then pour the mixture into the container of an ice cream machine and churn according to the manufacturer's instructions. Add the pistachios 5 minutes before the churning is completed. Transfer to an airtight container and freeze for at least 2 hours before serving.

Worth Its Weight in Gold

Saffron is the stigma of the *Crocus sativus*, a member of the Iris family. It is the world's most expensive spice—practically worth its weight in gold. Luckily you need to add only a small amount to dishes to impart saffron's brilliant yellow color and signature flavor. Some interesting facts:

- The word *saffron* derives from the Arab word *zafaran*, meaning "yellow," and it was mentioned as far back as 1500 B.C. in many classical writings as well as in the Bible.

- Saffron is native to Asia Minor, where it has been cultivated for thousands of years for use in medicines, perfumes, and as a flavoring for foods and beverages. Saffron once was used as a dye for the robes of Buddhist monks; its bright golden color symbolizes illumination.

- Saffron is considered an aphrodisiac, but large amounts can be toxic.

- It takes more than 70,000 flower buds and 210,000 threads (3 threads per flower) to make up a pound of saffron.

CHOCOLATE CHAI GELATO

In India there's a *chai walla*, or tea vendor, on every corner. We're not quite so lucky in the United States, but thanks to chai's universally appealing flavors and health benefits, it is becoming more and more popular in this country. The chai requires no brewing, so this gelato is a cinch to make.

Chocolate Base (page 25)

½ cup chai concentrate, such as Oregon Chai Concentrate

¼ cup heavy cream

Make the Chocolate Base and chill as directed.

Gently whisk the chai concentrate and cream into the base. Pour the mixture into the container of an ice cream machine and churn according to the manufacturer's instructions. Transfer to an airtight container and freeze for at least 2 hours before serving.

GREEK YOGURT GELATO

This light, tangy, and refreshing gelato was inspired by my travels in Syria, when I first tasted labne, a fresh cheese made from strained thick Greek-style yogurt that is used all over the Middle East. I was nineteen years old and it was love at first taste. In creating the flavor for the gelato I sought to keep the intense flavor of labne while maintaining its light structure.

You can find labne in Middle Eastern markets (Ciao Bella uses labne from Lebanon) and some gourmet groceries. Or you can easily make your own starting with Greek yogurt (make sure your yogurt doesn't contain stabilizers, such as pectin or gelatin, which will interfere with the thickening process). The labne increases the yield of this gelato to a bit more than 1 quart. —DZ

Plain Base (page 22)

⅔ cup labne (see below)

⅔ cup water

⅓ cup sugar

1 teaspoon fresh lemon juice

Make the Plain Base and chill as directed.

Place the labne in a medium bowl and slowly whisk in the water. Add the sugar and whisk until dissolved. Whisk in the lemon juice, then whisk the mixture into the base.

Pour the mixture into the container of an ice cream machine and churn according to the manufacturer's instructions. Transfer to an airtight container and freeze for at least 2 hours before serving.

LABNE

Just one ingredient goes into making labne. Keep in mind it will lose about half its volume.

2 cups Greek yogurt

Line a fine-mesh strainer with cheesecloth or a double layer of paper towels and set it over a bowl. In a separate small bowl, whisk the yogurt until smooth. Place in the colander and leave to drain in the refrigerator for 24 hours, stirring occasionally and pouring out the liquid from time to time. The labne should be thick and spreadable. Transfer to a container, cover, and refrigerate until ready to use.

Adults Only—Just about any

alcohol makes a great gelato; the creamy base mellows
the bite of the alcohol. Alcohol can slow the freezing
process, so these flavors don't freeze as hard as other
gelati. Make sure to keep all your ingredients very cold,
and store your gelato in the coldest part of your freezer.
Liqueur-based gelati are some of the easiest to make; in
many cases, mixing the spirit into the base is all that's
required. So open up your liquor cabinet and start
experimenting, with this one general guideline: Don't
exceed ¼ cup liquor per quart of gelato. Eat responsibly!

RUM RAISIN GELATO

Soaking the raisins overnight in the rum is the key to making this classic American flavor stand out. Use light rum, dark rum, or spiced rum—whichever you prefer; you can also experiment with other dried fruits such as figs or prunes. You'll need to macerate the raisins in the rum for twelve hours, so start this step the night before.

¼ cup raisins

½ cup rum

Plain Base (page 27)

Place the raisins and rum in a small bowl. Cover lightly with a clean kitchen towel and set aside at room temperature for 12 hours to macerate. Drain the raisins and refrigerate them. Reserve the rum.

Make the Plain Base and chill as directed.

Gently whisk the reserved rum into the base. Pour the mixture into the container of an ice cream machine and churn according to the manufacturer's instructions. Just after churning, stir in the raisins. Transfer to an airtight container and freeze for at least 2 hours before serving.

CHOCOLATE AMARETTO GELATO

For an extra indulgence try crumbling Amaretti cookies on top of this chocolate lovers' gelato. The sweetness of the Amaretto stands up beautifully to the intensity of the Chocolate Base, so you can use up to ½ cup Amaretto in this gelato.

Chocolate Base (page 25)

¼ to ½ cup Amaretto liqueur, chilled

Make the Chocolate Base and chill as directed.

Gently whisk the Amaretto into the base. Pour the mixture into the container of an ice cream machine and churn according to the manufacturer's instructions. Transfer to an airtight container and freeze for at least 2 hours before serving.

chocolate stout gelato, recipe opposite
irish cream gelato, recipe opposite
bourbon butter pecan gelato, page 115

CHOCOLATE STOUT GELATO

Beer and chocolate have become an increasingly popular pairing, and stouts and chocolate—both full-bodied—are natural partners. The beer cuts through the sweetness of the chocolate and the chocolate softens the bitterness of the beer. You can find malt powder near the dry milk products in your supermarket, or order it online (see Sources, page 174).

Chocolate Base (page 25)

1½ cups stout beer, such as Guinness

2 tablespoons malt powder

Make the Chocolate Base and chill as directed.

Pour the beer into a medium saucepan and place over medium-low heat. Bring to a simmer and simmer until reduced to 1 cup, watching the pan carefully so the beer doesn't boil over (take the pan off the heat immediately if it starts to bubble quickly and rise to the top). Remove the pan from the heat, and let cool completely. Transfer to a bowl, cover, and refrigerate until cold, about 1 hour.

Gently whisk the reduced beer and the malt powder into the base. Pour the mixture into the container of an ice cream machine and churn according to the manufacturer's instructions. Transfer to an airtight container and freeze for at least 2 hours before serving.

IRISH CREAM GELATO

For centuries the Irish have known to add cream to their whiskey to soften the effect of the alcohol and let the nutty, oaky flavors of the drink come through. Here we further smooth the flavor by adding this delicious liqueur to our gelato.

Plain Base (page 22)

¼ cup Irish Cream liqueur, such as Baileys, chilled

Make the Plain Base and chill as directed.

Gently whisk the Irish Cream into the base. Pour the mixture into the container of an ice cream machine and churn according to the manufacturer's instructions. Transfer to an airtight container and freeze for at least 2 hours before serving.

CARAMEL COGNAC GELATO

This French brandy–based gelato is an elegant way to enjoy our sensational caramel.

Plain Base (page 22)

¼ cup Caramel Sauce (page 55), at room temperature

¼ cup cognac, chilled

Make the Plain Base and chill as directed.

Gently whisk the caramel sauce and cognac into the base. Pour the mixture into the container of an ice cream machine and churn according to the manufacturer's instructions. Transfer to an airtight container and freeze for at least 2 hours before serving.

"**AS YOU CONTINUE** to explore the world of gelato, we leave you with this suggestion: Look beyond the sweet and obvious; experiment and be creative. Food, like any other art, reflects personality, individual expression, and mostly heart. If you don't bring passion and an open mind to the kitchen, you will never experience the joy of creation. The secret is to find the perfect balance and proportions, then let your ingredients come together, speak, and tell their story."

—CHEF DANILO

BOURBON BUTTER PECAN GELATO

This is a favorite with our steakhouse restaurant customers, who seem to crave a very grown-up version of our Butter Pecan Gelato (page 76). Photograph on page 112.

8 tablespoons (1 stick) unsalted butter

2 cups whole milk

1 cup heavy cream

⅔ cup sugar

4 large egg yolks

¼ cup bourbon

1 cup roasted pecan halves (see page 47), frozen

Place the butter in a small saucepan over medium heat. Heat, stirring frequently, until it melts completely and just turns a light golden, about 5 minutes. Remove from the heat, pour into a medium heat-proof bowl, and let cool slightly.

In a heavy-bottom saucepan, combine the milk and cream. Place over medium-low heat and cook, stirring occasionally so a skin doesn't form, until tiny bubbles start to form around the edges and the mixture reaches a temperature of 170°F.

Meanwhile, whisk the sugar with the butter until smooth, then whisk in the egg yolks until well incorporated and the mixture is thick and pale. Temper the egg yolks by very slowly pouring in the milk mixture while whisking continuously. Return the custard to the saucepan and place over low heat. Heat, stirring frequently with a wooden spoon, until thick enough to coat the back of the spoon and it reaches a temperature of 185°F. Do not bring to a boil.

Pour the custard through a fine-mesh strainer into a clean bowl and cool completely, stirring often. To cool the custard quickly, make an ice bath by filling a large bowl with ice and water and placing the bowl with the custard in it; stir the custard until cooled. Once completely cooled, cover and refrigerate until very cold, at least 4 hours or overnight.

Gently whisk the bourbon into the custard. Pour the mixture into the container of an ice cream machine and churn according to the manufacturer's instructions. Add the pecans 5 minutes before the churning is completed. Transfer to an airtight container and freeze for at least 2 hours before serving.

SORBETTO

Sorbetto is the Italian word for sorbet, which is the French word for "fruit ice." At Ciao Bella our interpretation is to puree fruit with just enough water and sugar to give this frozen dessert the perfect consistency. Sorbetto contains no dairy or eggs, so it is lighter than gelato, making it a delightfully refreshing culmination to any meal.

A simple syrup (see page 118) that can be made months in advance serves as the base for most of our sorbetti. When a different proportion of sugar is called for, we restate the simple syrup directions using the appropriate amount of sugar and water. Simple syrup can be put together in just a few minutes, so you can make any number of sorbetti at a moment's notice: Just blend your fruit, mix with the simple syrup, chill, and churn. The yield for the sorbetti in this chapter is approximately 1 quart, or 8 servings of sorbetto, depending on your ice cream maker and how ripe and juicy your fruit is.

Italians generally don't make a big distinction between gelato and sorbetto; instead they choose whatever flavor they're in the mood for. Italians also have a tradition of using tart sorbetto flavors, such as champagne or lemon, as palate cleansers between fish and meat courses or between strongly flavored dishes.

Cocktails also make wonderful sorbetto, and we've provided recipes for classics as well as some more experimental flavors. If it comes garnished with a paper parasol, Ciao Bella has more than likely made sorbetto out of it.

The section ends with instructions for making granita, a light and flavorful frozen dessert that doesn't require an ice cream maker.

SIMPLE SYRUP

Simple syrup, commonly used to sweeten sorbetti, bar drinks, and iced tea, is a mixture of water and sugar that's simmered until the sugar dissolves. While granulated sugar doesn't dissolve easily in cold liquids (when you try to stir sugar directly into iced tea, for example), simple syrup makes it easier to create sorbetto because it combines easily with fruit purees and other sorbetto ingredients. It keeps for months in a clean container in the refrigerator, so you can scale up the recipe and have a few batches on hand.

MAKES ABOUT 1⅓ CUPS

1 cup water

1 cup sugar

In a medium saucepan, combine the water and sugar. Place over medium-high heat and bring to a boil, whisking often to dissolve the sugar. Reduce the heat to medium-low and simmer for 4 minutes, while continuing to whisk until all the sugar is dissolved. Remove from the heat and let cool, then transfer to a bowl or container, cover, and refrigerate until cold, at least 1 hour.

FRESH MANGO SORBETTO

In Ciao Bella's early days, we used fresh imported mangos from the Caribbean for our sorbetto, but when we tried out a puree made from Indian Alphonso mangos, we discovered that they made incredibly flavorful sorbetto. Soon they became our mango of choice. If you are lucky enough to live in a warm climate where mangos are grown, you won't go wrong with fresh mangos. If not, using puree, which typically is made with mangos that are picked at their perfect ripeness, can be the best way of capturing their flavor and sweetness. Canned Alphonso mango puree can be found at Indian markets. Photograph on page 122.

4 large mangos, peeled and flesh cut into
   chunks (about 4 cups)

Simple Syrup (opposite)

In a blender, combine the mangos and simple syrup and blend until smooth. Pour the mixture into the container of an ice cream machine and churn according to the manu-facturer's instructions. Transfer to an airtight container and freeze for at least 2 hours before serving.

ALPHONSO MANGO SORBETTO

1 cup water

½ cup sugar

One 30-ounce can (3 cups) sweetened
   Alphonso mango puree, chilled

In a medium saucepan, combine the water and sugar. Place over medium-high heat and bring to a boil, whisking often to dissolve the sugar. Reduce the heat to medium-low and simmer for 4 minutes, while continuing to whisk until all the sugar is dissolved. Remove from the heat and let cool, then transfer to a bowl or container, cover, and refrigerate until cold, at least 1 hour.

Pour the simple syrup into the container of an ice cream machine, whisk in the mango puree, and churn according to the manufacturer's instructions. Transfer to an airtight container and freeze for at least 2 hours before serving.

BLOOD ORANGE SORBETTO

This is Ciao Bella's number-one-selling sorbetto. Its alluringly deep color and intensely aromatic citrus flavor have won it many fans, including Oprah Winfrey: The week she chose Blood Orange Sorbetto as one of her "Favorite Things," hits on our website jumped from 175,000 to 3 million.

3 cups blood orange juice (from about 15 medium blood oranges), chilled

1 tablespoon finely chopped grated blood orange zest

Simple Syrup (page 118)

In a large bowl, whisk together the juice, zest, and simple syrup. Pour the mixture into the container of an ice cream machine and churn according to the manufacturer's instructions. Transfer to an airtight container and freeze for at least 2 hours before serving.

Blood oranges are a deeply sweet and juicy orange variety with a striking orange-red flesh. Their characteristic blood color comes from a pigment called anthocyanin, a powerful antioxidant more common to flowers and other red fruits, particularly berries. Blood oranges also contain large amounts of vitamin C and fiber, making them extremely healthful. Tarocco blood oranges, native to Sicily, are what I use at Ciao Bella; they are refreshing, low in acidity, and the sweetest of the blood orange types.

Blood oranges are great for juicing; try using blood orange juice instead of regular orange juice in cocktails for an exciting presentation. The juice is also a great granita ingredient (see page 148). The blood orange is a classic Sicilian fruit; it reflects the nature and spirit of the Sicilian people: generous, direct, and unique. —DZ

RASPBERRY SORBETTO

At Ciao Bella, there's no skimping on the fruit in our sorbetti, and a total of six cups of berries go into a quart of our Raspberry Sorbetto. The result: a fragrant and sweet flavor with a subtly tart overtone, a striking fuchsia color, and a melt-in-your-mouth smooth texture. And as a bonus, you'll be getting a healthy amount of antioxidants and vitamin C.

6 cups fresh raspberries

1 teaspoon fresh lemon juice

Simple Syrup (page 118)

Place the raspberries and lemon juice in a food processor and puree until smooth, then pour into a fine-mesh strainer placed over a bowl, pressing on the solids to extract the raspberry puree. Discard the seeds.

Whisk the simple syrup into the raspberry puree, pour the mixture into the container of an ice cream machine, and churn according to the manufacturer's instructions. Transfer to an airtight container and freeze for at least 2 hours before serving.

FRAMBOISE LAMBIC BEER SORBETTO

Framboise is French for "raspberry," and Framboise Lambic beer is a Belgian brew that is fermented with raspberries. This beer has been gaining popularity in the United States in recent years, and it's a natural addition to our Raspberry Sorbetto. Recork the remaining beer and serve in wineglasses alongside your sorbetto.

Raspberry Sorbetto (at left)

1 cup Framboise Lambic beer

Make the base for the Raspberry Sorbetto as directed.

Pour the beer into a medium saucepan and place over medium heat. Bring to a boil, reduce the heat slightly, and boil for 1 minute (this evaporates some of the alcohol). Watch the pan carefully so the beer doesn't boil over (take the pan off the heat immediately if it starts to bubble quickly and rise to the top). Remove from the heat and let cool. Transfer to a bowl or container, cover, and refrigerate until cold, about 30 minutes.

Gently whisk the beer into the Raspberry Sorbetto base. Pour the mixture into the container of an ice cream machine and churn according to the manufacturer's instructions. Transfer to an airtight container and freeze for at least 2 hours before serving.

LEMON SORBETTO

Lemon was one of the first sorbetto flavors to come out of Italy, and to this day it is the favorite of Italians. At restaurants it is often served as a palate cleanser, or *intermezzo* ("between courses"). There are many variations on Lemon Sorbetto, with additional ingredients such as basil, thyme, or grappa, a brandy made from the skins and seeds of grapes.

At Ciao Bella our Lemon Sorbetto uses fragrant, tart, and juicy Femminello lemons from Sicily. They are recognized the world over for their exceptional flavor, and the oil found in the skin gives a unique perfume to the fruit. Photograph on page 122.

1 cup fresh lemon juice (from about 6 large lemons), strained and chilled

2 recipes Simple Syrup (page 118)

1 tablespoon finely chopped grated lemon zest

In the container of an ice cream machine, whisk together the juice, simple syrup, and zest and churn according to the manufacturer's instructions. Transfer to an airtight container and freeze for at least 2 hours before serving.

CANTALOUPE SORBETTO

The cantaloupe was named after the Cantalupo area of Italy, near Tivoli, the summer residence of the pope. Its sweet, musky flavor and soft texture make it a natural for sorbetto—the riper the melon the better. Just about any kind of melon will work, so feel free to try different types; your farmers' market is a good place to find local varieties.

1 large cantaloupe, cut in half, seeded, flesh cut from skin and chopped (about 4 cups)

1 tablespoon fresh lemon juice

Simple Syrup (page 118)

In a blender, combine the cantaloupe, lemon juice, and simple syrup and blend until smooth. Pour the mixture into the container of an ice cream machine and churn according to the manufacturer's instructions. Transfer to an airtight container and freeze for at least 2 hours before serving.

CANTALOUPE TARRAGON SORBETTO

Make the Cantaloupe Sorbetto above, adding 2 tablespoons minced fresh tarragon just before churning.

HONEYDEW SORBETTO

Substitute 1 small honeydew for the cantaloupe and proceed as above.

PEACH SORBETTO

This summer crowd-pleaser is best made with seasonal fresh fruit and offers a great use for overripe fruit. White peaches are traditional in Italy, but any sweet and juicy peach will make a great sorbetto.

2½ pounds (about 5 large) peaches
2 teaspoons fresh lemon juice
Simple Syrup (page 118)

Bring a large saucepan of water to a boil. Using the tip of a paring knife, cut a small X into the bottom of the peaches. Immerse the peaches in the boiling water and blanch for about 1 minute to loosen the skins (the riper the peach, the less time required). Using a slotted spoon, remove the peaches, immediately plunge them into a bowl filled with ice water, and let them sit until cool enough to handle, about 1 minute. Peel the peaches using a paring knife, then remove the pit and roughly chop the flesh.

Place the peach flesh and lemon juice in a food processor and puree until smooth, scraping down the sides of the machine once or twice if needed. Pour through a fine-mesh strainer into a bowl, pressing down on the solids to extract all the liquid. Discard the solids. Cover and refrigerate until cold, about 1 hour.

Whisk the simple syrup into the peach puree, then pour the mixture into the container of an ice cream machine and churn according to the manufacturer's instructions. Transfer to an airtight container and freeze for at least 2 hours before serving.

PEACH AND HABANERO SORBETTO

The sweet, delicate complexity of ripe peaches with the intense heat of habanero chiles is not for everybody, but it's an incredible combination for the adventurous palate.

Make the Peach Sorbetto above, adding a pinch of ground dried habanero chile (see Sources, page 174) just before churning.

Our recipe tester, Leda Scheintaub, author of *Chipotle: Smoky Hot Recipes for All Occasions*, recommends making your own chile powder. It's easy to do, and the flavor of just-ground chile powder is unmistakable.

Preheat a skillet over medium heat. Add the chiles two at a time and toast, pressing down on them with the back of a spatula, until lightly browned, 10 to 20 seconds per side, then let cool. Remove the stems and seeds and crumble the chiles (wear plastic gloves). In a spice grinder or a food processor, blend until a fine powder forms. Let the chile powder settle, then transfer to an airtight container.

WATERMELON SORBETTO

Watermelon contains less sugar by weight than you might think: only 6 percent. It tastes much sweeter because the sugar is its primary flavor-producing element; the rest is mostly water, which is why it's a cool summer favorite. Use seedless watermelon when you can find it, or remove the seeds before blending. Experiment with yellow or orange watermelon when available.

6 cups chopped seedless watermelon (from a 2-pound piece of watermelon)

2 tablespoons fresh lemon juice

Simple Syrup (page 118)

In a blender, combine the watermelon, lemon juice, and simple syrup and blend until smooth. Pour the mixture into the container of an ice cream machine and churn according to the manufacturer's instructions. Transfer to an airtight container and freeze for at least 2 hours before serving.

WATERMELON MINT SORBETTO

For an extra-refreshing variation, make the Watermelon Sorbetto above, adding 2 tablespoons minced fresh mint just before churning.

PEAR SORBETTO

People often remark that this sorbetto tastes just like eating a pear. We call for the Bartlett variety; if unavailable, any type of pear will work well. Use the softest pears you can find, preferably ripe and in season. If the pears aren't fully ripened, you will need to cook them a little longer.

½ lemon

3 pounds (about 5 large) ripe Bartlett pears

2 cups water

1 cup sugar

¼ cup white wine

1 teaspoon grated lemon zest

Fill a large bowl with cold water. Squeeze 1 tablespoon of juice from the lemon and set aside. Squeeze the rest of the lemon juice into the water and toss in the lemon half. Peel, core, and chop the pears, placing the pear pieces in the lemon water as you chop to keep them from browning.

In a large saucepan, combine the 2 cups water and the sugar. Add the reserved lemon juice to the pan. Place over medium heat and bring to a boil, whisking often to dissolve the sugar. Reduce the heat to medium-low and simmer for 4 minutes, continuing to whisk until all the sugar is dissolved. Whisk in the wine and lemon zest, then add the pears. Lower the heat, and simmer until the pears are soft and the syrup is thick, about 30 minutes. Remove

from the heat and let cool completely. Transfer to a large bowl and mash with a potato masher until fairly smooth with a few small pear chunks remaining. Transfer to a bowl, cover, and refrigerate until cold, at least 4 hours.

Pour the mixture into the container of an ice cream machine and churn according to the manufacturer's instructions. Transfer to an airtight container and freeze for at least 2 hours before serving.

PEAR SORBETTO WITH BALSAMIC SWIRL

If you are open to untraditional sorbetto flavor combinations, this variation on Pear Sorbetto with a swirl of tart balsamic vinegar syrup is for you.

Make the Pear Sorbetto above; just after churning, gradually squeeze ½ cup Balsamic Vinegar Syrup (page 66) from a squeeze bottle over the top of the sorbetto and quickly and lightly swirl in a zigzag pattern with a spoon or butter knife. Alternatively, transfer one third of the sorbetto to the container you're freezing it in and squeeze one third (about 2 tablespoons) of the syrup over it. Repeat layering with the remaining sorbetto and syrup, then freeze for at least 2 hours before serving.

KIWI SORBETTO

Brilliant green, this sorbetto captures the unique sweet and slightly tart flavor of the kiwi, and the little black seeds provide a nice crunch. Mashing the kiwis by hand rather than blending them helps preserve their beautiful color, but if you like your sorbetto super-smooth, you can blend without any loss of flavor.

8 kiwis, peeled and roughly chopped

1 tablespoon fresh lemon juice

Simple Syrup (page 118)

In a large bowl, combine the kiwis, lemon juice, and simple syrup, and mash with a potato masher until fairly smooth with a few small kiwi chunks remaining. Pour the mixture into the container of an ice cream machine and churn according to the manufacturer's instructions. Transfer to an airtight container and freeze for at least 2 hours before serving.

STRAWBERRY SORBETTO

At Ciao Bella, we make our Strawberry Sorbetto with Pacific Northwest strawberries picked at the height of ripeness—super-sweet and juicy red all the way through. Make this in the summer with locally grown strawberries for maximum flavor and freshness.

2 cups water

1½ cups sugar

2 quarts fresh strawberries, hulled and quartered

1 tablespoon fresh lemon juice

In a medium saucepan, combine the water and sugar. Place over medium-high heat and bring to a boil, whisking often to dissolve the sugar. Reduce the heat to medium-low and simmer for 4 minutes, while continuing to whisk until all the sugar is dissolved. Remove from the heat and let cool. Transfer to a bowl or container, cover, and refrigerate until cold, at least 1 hour.

In a blender, combine 1 quart of the strawberries, ½ tablespoon of the lemon juice, and half of the simple syrup, and blend until smooth. Pour the mixture into the container of an ice cream machine. Blend the remaining strawberries, lemon juice, and simple syrup, whisk into the container, and churn according to the manufacturer's instructions. Transfer to an airtight container and freeze for at least 2 hours before serving.

kiwi sorbetto, recipe opposite
cosmopolitan sorbetto, page 141
raspberry sorbetto, page 123

CHOCOLATE SORBETTO

Our Chocolate Sorbetto is incredibly rich and velvety; without any added cream its perfect chocolate goodness comes through clear and true. It's rich in flavor but light in texture, making it an elegant finish to a meal. As with gelato, you might like to try different origins and percentages of chocolate to vary your experience (see page 30). Try topping it with raspberries, pairing it with Raspberry Sorbetto (page 123), or garnishing it with a few chocolate-covered cacao nibs (see Sources, page 174).

3 cups water

1½ cups sugar

4 ounces bittersweet chocolate (about 60% cacao), finely chopped

½ cup unsweetened cocoa powder

1 teaspoon dark rum

¼ teaspoon pure vanilla extract

In a medium saucepan, combine the water and sugar. Place over medium-high heat and bring to a boil, whisking often to dissolve the sugar. Reduce the heat to medium-low and simmer for 4 minutes, continuing to whisk until all the sugar is dissolved.

Remove the pan from the heat and add the chopped chocolate; whisk until the chocolate is completely melted. Add the cocoa powder and whisk until incorporated and the mixture

is smooth. Add the rum and vanilla, then pour through a fine-mesh strainer into a clean bowl. Let cool completely, stirring often. To cool quickly, make an ice bath by filling a large bowl with ice and water and placing the bowl with the mixture in it; stir the mixture until cooled. Once completely cooled, cover and refrigerate until very cold, at least 4 hours or overnight.

Pour the mixture into the container of an ice cream machine and churn according to the manufacturer's instructions. Transfer to an airtight container and freeze for at least 2 hours before serving.

CHOCOLATE ORANGE SORBETTO

Make the Chocolate Sorbetto above, omitting the rum and vanilla extract. Add ⅛ teaspoon orange extract and 1 teaspoon finely chopped grated orange zest just before churning.

COCONUT LEMONGRASS SORBETTO

This Asian-inspired sorbetto takes its cue from a classic Thai flavor combination. The intensity of the coconut is balanced with the light herbal citrus flavor of the lemongrass. You'll find lemongrass in the produce section in Asian markets and at some supermarkets.

1¾ cups water

1 cup sugar

1 cup finely chopped fresh lemongrass, white parts only (from about 10 peeled stalks)

One 14-ounce can (1¾ cups) unsweetened coconut milk (not light)

In a medium saucepan, combine the water, sugar, and lemongrass. Bring to a boil over medium-high heat, whisking to dissolve the sugar, then reduce the heat to medium-low, cover, and simmer for 40 minutes. Remove from the heat, and pour through a fine-mesh strainer into a heat-proof bowl, pressing on the solids to extract all the liquid. Discard the lemongrass, then whisk in the coconut milk. Pour into a bowl and let cool completely. Cover and refrigerate until very cold, at least 4 hours or overnight.

Pour the mixture into the container of an ice cream machine and churn according to the manufacturer's instructions. Transfer to an airtight container and freeze for at least 2 hours before serving.

LEMON VERBENA SORBETTO

Known for its calming effects, lemon verbena, the queen of lemon-scented herbs, has a uniquely rich but mellow lemon flavor. Fresh lemon juice is added to make this sorbetto both soothing and refreshing. Fresh berries are the perfect topping.

3 cups water

1½ cups sugar

¼ cup dried lemon verbena (see Sources, page 174)

6 tablespoons fresh lemon juice, strained and chilled

In a medium saucepan, combine the water and sugar. Place over medium-high heat and bring to a boil, whisking often to dissolve the sugar. Reduce the heat to medium-low and simmer for 4 minutes, while continuing to whisk until all the sugar is dissolved.

Add the lemon verbena to the simple syrup, cover, and set aside to steep for 20 minutes. Strain into a bowl or container, pressing on the solids to extract all the liquid. Discard the solids. Let cool to room temperature, then cover and refrigerate until cold, about 1 hour.

Whisk the lemon juice into the mixture, pour into the container of an ice cream machine, and churn according to the manufacturer's instructions. Transfer to an airtight container and freeze for at least 2 hours before serving.

Ciao Bella's NASFT Award–Winning Flavors

Each year the National Association for the Specialty Food Trade, a nonprofit business trade association, recognizes the best of the best in the food industry with its prestigious sofi awards. Formerly known as the NASFT Product Awards, the sofi awards is a competition held every spring to recognize outstanding specialty food products. There are thirty categories and about a thousand retailers and food service professionals from around the country vote on each category. These Ciao Bella favorites have all been winners:

Tahitian Vanilla Gelato (page 27)

Pistachio Gelato (page 47)

Key Lime with Graham Cracker Gelato (page 69)

Hazelnut Biscotti Gelato (page 78)

Fresh Mint Gelato (page 98)

Greek Yogurt Gelato (page 109)

Fresh Mango Sorbetto (page 119)

Blood Orange Sorbetto (page 120)

Raspberry Sorbetto (page 123)

Chocolate Sorbetto (page 133)

Blackberry Cabernet Sorbetto (page 143)

COCONUT SORBETTO

Our deliciously refreshing and clean-tasting Coconut Sorbetto is both light and surprisingly rich and creamy. It's one of the few sorbetti that contain fat (though no dairy, so it's suitable for vegans), but it's a healthful fat that contains high amounts of lauric acid, an antiviral agent that strengthens the immune system and boosts brain function. Try serving it with Fresh Mango Sorbetto (page 119) for a tropical pairing. It's also perfect with Chocolate Sorbetto (page 133).

One 14-ounce can (1¾ cups) unsweetened coconut milk (not light)

1¼ cups water

1 cup sugar

¼ cup sweetened shredded dried coconut

In a medium saucepan, combine the coconut milk, water, and sugar. Place over medium heat and bring to a simmer, whisking often to dissolve the sugar. Reduce the heat to medium-low and simmer for 4 minutes, continuing to whisk until all the sugar is dissolved. Pour into a bowl and let cool completely.

To cool quickly, make an ice bath by filling a large bowl with ice and water and placing the bowl with the mixture in it; stir until the mixture is cooled. Once completely cooled, cover and refrigerate until very cold, at least 4 hours or overnight.

Stir the shredded coconut into the mixture. Pour into the container of an ice cream machine and churn according to the manufacturer's instructions. Transfer to an airtight container and freeze for at least 2 hours before serving.

COCONUT WITH CARAMEL SWIRL SORBETTO

Make the Coconut Sorbetto above; just after churning gradually squeeze ½ cup Caramel Sauce (page 55) from a squeeze bottle over the top of the sorbetto and quickly and lightly swirl in a zigzag pattern with a spoon or butter knife. Alternatively, transfer one third of the sorbetto to the container you're freezing it in and squeeze one third (about 2 tablespoons) of the caramel over it. Repeat layering with the remaining sorbetto and caramel, then freeze for at least 2 hours before serving.

POMEGRANATE CHAMPAGNE SORBETTO

Native to Iran, this ancient fruit is rich in history and is often referred to in the Bible. In Greek mythology it is associated with Persephone, goddess of fertility and the underworld, and thus the many-seeded pomegranate has come to symbolize fecundity, death, and the everlasting. The pomegranate has traditionally been an important part of the Middle Eastern diet, and in recent years it has reached superfruit status in this country because of its high antioxidant and vitamin content. In this sorbetto the characteristic sweet and tart flavor of the pomegranate juice mellows the kick of the champagne—what better way to toast to your health?

1½ cups pomegranate juice

1 cup champagne, chilled

Simple Syrup (page 118)

¼ teaspoon fresh lemon juice

In a large bowl, whisk together the pomegranate juice, champagne, simple syrup, and lemon juice. Pour the mixture into the container of an ice cream machine and churn according to the manufacturer's instructions. Transfer to an airtight container and freeze for at least 2 hours before serving.

CHAMPAGNE SORBETTO

Although many of us think of sorbetto as a hot-weather dessert, New Year's Eve is often Ciao Bella's biggest-selling sorbetto day of the year. That's when New York City restaurants ring in the new with Champagne Sorbetto, served between courses as a distinctive—and festive—palate cleanser. There's more than a hint of champagne here, so we recommend that you serve small portions, or pair it with a sweet fruit sorbetto.

1 large egg white (see Note)

2 cups champagne, chilled

Simple Syrup (page 118)

¼ teaspoon fresh lemon juice

In a medium bowl, beat the egg white until soft peaks just begin to form.

Pour the champagne into a separate bowl. Slowly whisk in the egg white until incorporated, then slowly whisk in the simple syrup and lemon juice.

Pour the mixture into the container of an ice cream machine and churn according to the manufacturer's instructions. Transfer to an airtight container and freeze for at least 2 hours before serving.

NOTE
If raw eggs are a concern, use pasteurized egg whites.

BELLINI SORBETTO

This sorbetto takes its cue from the peach and prosecco cocktail invented in the 1930s by Giuseppe Cipriani of Harry's Bar in Venice—a famous haunt of Ernest Hemingway and Humphrey Bogart, among other celebrities. The Bellini quickly became a classic and is now one of Italy's most popular mixed drinks. It makes great use of leftover prosecco or champagne—perfect for your New Year's Day brunch menu.

1½ pounds (about 3 large) fresh peaches

1 teaspoon fresh lemon juice

Simple Syrup (page 118)

1 cup champagne or prosecco, chilled

Bring a large saucepan of water to a boil. Using the tip of a paring knife, cut a small X into the bottom of the peaches. Immerse the peaches in the boiling water and blanch for about 1 minute to loosen the skins (the riper the peach, the less time required). Using a slotted spoon, remove the peaches, immediately plunge them into a bowl filled with ice water, and let them sit until cool enough to handle, about 1 minute. Peel the peaches using a paring knife, then remove the pit and roughly chop the flesh.

Place the peach flesh and lemon juice in a food processor and puree until smooth, scraping down the sides of the machine once or twice if needed. Pour through a fine-mesh strainer into a bowl, pressing down on the solids to extract all the liquid. Discard the solids. Cover and refrigerate until cold, about 1 hour.

Whisk the simple syrup into the peach puree, then gently whisk in the champagne. Pour the mixture into the container of an ice cream machine and churn according to the manufacturer's instructions. Transfer to an airtight container and freeze for at least 2 hours before serving.

COSMOPOLITAN SORBETTO

This refreshing, pretty-in-pink cooler is nice in our Festa Limonata drink (page 171).

2 cups water

1½ cups sugar

2 cups fresh or frozen cranberries

¼ cup fresh lime juice, strained and chilled

¼ cup fresh lemon juice, strained and chilled

¼ cup vodka, chilled

1 tablespoon Cointreau or Triple Sec

In a medium saucepan, combine the water and sugar. Bring to a boil over medium-high heat, whisking often to dissolve the sugar. Reduce the heat and simmer for 4 minutes, continuing to whisk until all the sugar is dissolved. Remove from the heat and set aside.

Bring a medium saucepan of water to a boil. Add the cranberries, return to a boil, then simmer over medium-low until the skins start to pop, about 10 minutes. Drain, transfer to a blender, add the syrup, and blend until smooth. Let cool, transfer to a bowl, cover, and refrigerate, at least 4 hours.

Add the lime juice, lemon juice, vodka, and Cointreau and stir to combine. Pour into the container of an ice cream machine and churn according to the manufacturer's instructions. Transfer to an airtight container and freeze for at least 2 hours before serving.

CHERRY SAKE SORBETTO

We created this sweet sake-based flavor for a Japanese restaurant in California. They didn't wind up placing an order for it, but we liked it so much that we kept it on as a seasonal flavor and it has been popular with customers ever since.

1½ pounds fresh sweet cherries, pitted

2 teaspoons fresh lemon juice

Simple Syrup (page 118)

½ cup sake, chilled

Place the cherries and lemon juice in a food processor and puree until smooth, scraping down the sides of the machine once or twice if needed. Pour into a bowl and whisk in the simple syrup and sake. Pour the mixture into the container of an ice cream machine and churn according to the manufacturer's instructions, then transfer to an airtight container and freeze for at least 2 hours before serving.

BLACKBERRY CABERNET SORBETTO

Tart and sweet blackberries play off dark, tannic, full-bodied cabernet in a sophisticated flavor combination. This elegant sorbetto has attracted a lot of press attention, became the number-one-selling sorbetto in our San Francisco store, and won a sofi award. To make Blackberry Sorbetto without the wine, simply omit the cabernet.

2 cups cabernet sauvignon

6 cups fresh blackberries

1 tablespoon fresh lemon juice

Simple Syrup (page 118)

Pour the wine into a medium saucepan and place over medium heat. Simmer until reduced to 1 cup, about 10 minutes. Remove from the heat, and let cool completely. Transfer to a bowl, cover, and refrigerate until cold, about 1 hour.

Place the blackberries and lemon juice in a food processor and puree until smooth, then pour into a fine-mesh strainer placed over a bowl, pressing on the solids to extract the blackberry puree. Discard the seeds.

Whisk the wine and simple syrup into the blackberry puree, pour the mixture into the container of an ice cream machine, and churn according to the manufacturer's instructions. Transfer to an airtight container and freeze for at least 2 hours before serving.

" **WHEN I TURNED SIXTEEN** and was allowed to have a little wine, my mother made a dessert with fresh blackberries from our garden sprinkled with sugar and a drop of lemon, then drizzled with a full-bodied red wine. This fantastic combination was absolutely explosive, *paradiso in terra* (heaven on earth). Whenever I have a scoop of Blackberry Cabernet Sorbetto—my favorite flavor—it brings me back to this moment. "

—CHEF DANILO

GRAPEFRUIT CAMPARI SORBETTO

Ciao Bella has made this classic Italian flavor since the beginning, and it's the favorite of our president, Charlie Apt. Campari, invented in the 1860s by Gaspare Campari, is an alcoholic beverage made with a secret mixture of herbs and bark that gives it its characteristic bitter edge. Here that bitterness is intensified by the sharpness of the grapefruit, which makes this the quintessential palate cleanser; if you want to serve it as a dessert, increase the sugar to 2 cups. Campari's distinctive red color lends a beautiful gentle pink tone to the sorbetto. For a non-alcoholic grapefruit sorbetto, simply omit the Campari.

3 cups fresh grapefruit juice (from about 4 large grapefruits), strained and chilled

1½ cups sugar

½ cup Campari, chilled

In a blender, combine the grapefruit juice and sugar, and blend until the sugar is dissolved. Add the Campari, pour the mixture into the container of an ice cream machine, and churn according to the manufacturer's instructions. Transfer to an airtight container and freeze for at least 2 hours before serving.

Granita

—a slushy frozen mixture usually flavored with fruit or coffee—hails from Sicily but is enjoyed all over Italy. It's often served in a plastic cup with a straw or for breakfast with brioche. It doesn't require an ice cream maker and is endlessly versatile. Here, we'll share a basic recipe for a beloved granita flavor; and then we encourage you, as usual, to experiment.

RASPBERRY GRANITA

MAKES ABOUT 1½ QUARTS

6 cups fresh raspberries (to equal 2 cups
puree)

1 teaspoon fresh lemon juice

2 cups water

½ cup sugar, or to taste

Place the raspberries and lemon juice in a
food processor and puree until smooth, then
pour into a fine-mesh strainer placed over a
bowl, pressing on the solids to extract the
raspberry puree. Discard the seeds. Add the
water and sugar and whisk until the sugar is
dissolved.

Pour the mixture into a 9 by 12-inch baking
dish and place in the freezer. Freeze for 3 to
4 hours, stirring with a fork every 30 minutes
to break up the ice crystals, until the granita
is almost completely frozen and the texture is
like shaved ice. To serve, scrape the surface of
the granita with a fork or ice cream scooper to
create shaved crystals. Scoop into chilled
glasses and serve immediately.

GRANITA VARIATIONS

We've provided a chart on the following
page with flavor combinations to get you
started, but we hope you'll experiment a little
to come up with your own signature granita.

MAKES ABOUT 1½ QUARTS

In a medium bowl, combine your chosen
ingredients and whisk until the sweetener is
dissolved. Pour the mixture into a 9 by 12-inch
baking dish and place in the freezer. Freeze
for 3 to 4 hours, stirring with a fork every 30
minutes to break up the ice crystals, until the
granita is almost completely frozen and the
texture is like shaved ice. To serve, scrape the
surface of the granita with a fork or ice cream
scooper to create shaved crystals. Scoop into
chilled glasses and serve immediately.

These are a few of our favorite granita flavor combinations:

Pear • Grappa • Sugar • Lemon juice
Blood orange • Tequila • Sugar • Lemon juice
Peach • Prosecco • Sugar • Lemon juice
Blueberry • Pomegranate juice • Sugar • Lime juice

For more ideas, see the mix-and-match chart below. Feel free to choose one (or more) items from each column. There are also a few general rules to help you perfect your own flavors:

- If you're using citrus fruits such as lemons or grapefruit, increase the amount of sweetener.

- If you're using juice or a sweet wine as your liquid, use less sweetener.

- Honey, maple syrup, and agave nectar are sweeter than sugar, so use a little less than ½ cup and reduce the amount of liquid slightly.

FRUIT / FLAVOR	LIQUID	SWEETENER	OTHER FLAVORINGS
2 cups	2 cups	Up to ½ cup	To taste
Peaches	Water	Sugar	Lemon or lime juice
Raspberries	White wine	Honey	Lemon or lime zest
Blackberries	Red wine	Maple syrup	Orange zest
Lemon	Dessert wine (such as Sauternes or Vin Santo)	Agave nectar	Balsamic vinegar
Grapefruit	Prosecco		Rosewater
Blood orange	Tequila		Black pepper
Melon	Grappa		Cinnamon
Pear	Pomegranate juice		Mint
Blueberry	Orange juice		Basil
Coffee/espresso			

AFTERNOON REFRESHMENTS &
AMAZING ENDINGS

G elato and sorbetto are the perfect ending
to any meal, either served unadorned, in
simple perfection, or dressed up for a
distinctive dessert experience. In this chapter we've offered
a few plating suggestions to get you started (and of course,
we hope you'll be inspired to adopt the many others you've
seen in the photographs throughout this book); a recipe for
gelato truffles that will bring you rave reviews; and gelato and
sorbetto cakes for special celebrations. Fruit soups and salads are a
light finish to any meal, and gelato sandwiches are fun to make and
offer endless variations. And the drinks—shakes, smoothies, and tea- and
coffee-based brews—will cool you down in the summer and comfort you in
the winter. No matter how you serve them, gelato and sorbetto make any
occasion a festive one.

Simple Yet Creative Presentations—There are

so many ways to showcase gelato and sorbetto—be they as simple as a fruit, nut, or syrup topping, or as elaborate as putting together a tasting party with bold cutting-edge flavors. Here are some ideas to get your creative juices flowing.

Ciao Bella's Top Ten Unique Serving Suggestions

1. **INSTEAD OF JUST SPRINKLING DRY TOPPINGS, ROLL THE WHOLE SCOOP IN THEM.** Try chopped peanuts, sprinkles, shredded coconut, or mini chocolate chips.

2. **INDULGE IN A BROWNIE SUNDAE.** Try Eleni's Fudgy Walnut Brownies (page 49) topped with a scoop of gelato and Chocolate Sauce (page 154).

3. **MAKE AN ARTISTIC SAMPLER.** Try a painter's palette. Fill a squeeze bottle with Chocolate Sauce (page 154) and with the sauce draw a palette on a large white plate. Place five or six different-colored gelati and sorbetti within the border of the palette (for paint), and garnish with a rolled cookie or ladyfinger (for brushes). Or use different-colored pools of coulis (see page 158) to fill out the palette.

4. **CREATE WHIMSICAL SHAPES WITH SILICONE MUFFIN MOLDS.** Fill the molds with softened gelato, freeze, then unmold and serve. Try heart-shaped molds filled with Strawberry Gelato (page 64), flower-shaped molds with Rose Petal Gelato (page 97), or gingerbread people molds with Ginger Gelato (page 101).

5. **BRING OUT THE CRYSTAL.** Try a fancy ice bucket filled with two quarts of gelato for a special occasion; scoop the gelato into wineglasses at the table.

6. **FORGET ICE CREAM BOWLS.** Try untraditional serving dishes such as egg cups, soy sauce dishes, or champagne glasses.

7. **RELEASE YOUR INNER MONDRIAN OR POLLOCK:** Try a white dessert plate decorated with fruit coulis (see page 158); use the coulis squeeze bottles to go wild with swirls, stripes, and polka dots of contrasting colors.

8. **PUT YOUR OLD COLLEGE SHOT GLASSES TO USE.** Try flights of gelato or sorbetto; line up the shot glasses and serve a selection of flavors from our Adults Only section (pages 110–115).

9. **SERVE A MEDLEY OF SMALL SCOOPS.** Try an assortment of flavors, each in its own tiny dish and scooped with a melon baller; place the dishes on a platter for your guests to choose from (or present each person with a small platter topped with four tiny dishes of various flavors).

10. **END WITH A DRIZZLE.** Try Balsamic Vinegar Syrup (page 66) over Strawberry Gelato (page 64) or vanilla gelato (pages 26–27), or Caramel Sauce (page 55) or Chocolate Sauce (page 154) on just about any flavor.

THE PEARCE PARFAIT

This old-fashioned dessert is based on a treat I grew up with and enjoyed twenty years before my involvement with Ciao Bella. It was a favorite of my father's; he enjoyed the simple pleasures of life. We made this with vanilla ice cream, chocolate sauce, and peanut brittle; I encourage you to experiment with the other gelato flavors, candies, and sauces that you find throughout this book.
—FW

SERVES 2

6 scoops vanilla gelato (see pages 26–27)

Walnut Pralines (page 72) or peanut brittle, broken into pieces

Chocolate Sauce (at right)

Whipped cream (optional)

Place one scoop of gelato in each of 2 parfait or pilsner glasses. Top with some Walnut Praline, then drizzle with chocolate sauce. Repeat twice, ending with chocolate sauce; top with a dollop of whipped cream, if using.

CHOCOLATE SAUCE
MAKES ABOUT 2 CUPS

1 cup water

½ cup sugar

½ cup light corn syrup

¾ cup unsweetened cocoa powder

2 ounces bittersweet chocolate (about 60% cacao), finely chopped

In a medium saucepan, whisk together the water, sugar, and corn syrup, then whisk in the cocoa powder. Place over medium heat and bring to a boil, whisking constantly. Remove from the heat, add the chopped chocolate, and whisk until completely melted. Let cool, then transfer to a container, cover, and refrigerate. The sauce will keep for up to 2 weeks.

CARAMELIZED BANANA SUNDAE

The classic banana split is made with vanilla, chocolate, and strawberry; it is pictured on page 73 with Banana with Walnut Praline Gelato, but you can use any flavor or flavors you like. Banana Cajeta Cashew Gelato (page 92) and Dulce de Leche Gelato (page 105) are great choices.

SERVES 2

¼ cup light brown sugar

2 ripe bananas, cut in half lengthwise

6 scoops gelato

Chocolate Sauce (page 154)

Whipped cream (optional)

Preheat the broiler.

Spread the brown sugar out on a large plate and dip the cut sides of the bananas in the sugar. Place on a rimmed baking sheet, sugar side up, and broil until caramelized, 1 to 2 minutes.

Divide the banana halves between 2 bowls or sundae dishes, top each with 3 scoops of gelato, and drizzle with chocolate sauce. Top with whipped cream, if using.

The Scoop on Ice Cream Scoopers

Some ice cream scoopers are marked with a number; this number corresponds to the number of scoops in a quart. Most are #8 portion-control scoops, meaning they will measure about 8 scoops per quart, which is 4 ounces, or ½ cup. Using inverse logic, the larger the number, the smaller the actual scoop, so a #16 scooper will yield about 16 scoops per quart. If your scooper doesn't have a number on it, to figure out how much it holds, fill the scooper with water, then pour the water into a measuring cup. Your actual scoop will be double the size after you turn it into a perfectly formed scoop of gelato. For example, if your scooper holds 2 ounces, or ¼ cup of water, your resulting scoop will be 4 ounces, or ½ cup.

A Well-Dressed Plate

—This is one of the techniques chefs at fine restaurants use to wow us: Make a pool of crème anglaise in the center of a salad plate. Make a slightly smaller pool of chocolate sauce in the center of the crème anglaise. Using the tip of a paring knife or a toothpick, pull the sauces toward the edge of the plate; repeat several times to create a starburst pattern. Top with scoops of Classic Chocolate Gelato (page 28) or Coffee Gelato (page 50) or any of your favorites. (Crème Fraîche Gelato, page 90, is also an excellent choice.) For sorbetto, substitute mango coulis and raspberry coulis for the sauces and top with scoops of fruit sorbetto of any flavor.

RASPBERRY COULIS

MAKES ABOUT ½ CUP

2 cups raspberries

2 tablespoons sugar

1 teaspoon fresh lemon juice

Place the raspberries, sugar, and lemon juice in a food processor and puree until smooth and the sugar is dissolved. Pour into a fine-mesh strainer placed over a bowl, pressing on the solids to extract the raspberry puree. Discard the seeds. Transfer to a bowl or container, cover, and refrigerate until ready to serve.

MANGO COULIS

MAKES ABOUT ½ CUP

1 medium mango, peeled and flesh cut into chunks (about 1 cup)

1 tablespoon water, or as needed

2 tablespoons sugar

½ teaspoon fresh lemon juice

Place the mango, water, sugar, and lemon juice in a food processor and puree until smooth and the sugar is dissolved, adding water as needed for a thick but pourable consistency. Transfer to a bowl or container, cover, and refrigerate until ready to serve.

A Colorful Touch

Coulis, a thick sauce usually made from pureed fruit, adds a flash of color and a burst of flavor to any gelato presentation. Chefs love to use coulis because it's simple to make and dramatic to serve. Taste your coulis for sweetness; depending on the ripeness of the fruit you may need more sugar or lemon juice to achieve the correct balance.

GELATO TRUFFLES

Chocolate truffles, or *tartufo* in Italian, get their name from their resemblance to the black fungus famous around the world for its unique taste. Playful yet sophisticated, gelato truffles are a great make-ahead dessert. Our recipe is for large truffles, but you can create truffles of any size or flavor; use a melon baller for small scoops and pick them up with a toothpick or place them in decorative foil cups.

Some flavor ideas: Try Peppermint Stick Gelato (page 85) for the holidays, Rose Petal Gelato (page 97) for Mother's Day, or the classic Italian Tartufo, made with chocolate gelato (see page 28) and vanilla gelato (see pages 26–27) and with a cherry and a hazelnut in the middle (press the cherry and hazelnut into the center while the gelato is still in the scooper). Another option is to roll the still-wet truffles in complementary chopped nuts, such as Hazelnut Gelato (page 39) with chopped roasted hazelnuts or Butter Pecan Gelato (page 76) with chopped roasted pecans.

MAKES 10 TRUFFLES

1 quart gelato

Chocolate Ganache (recipe follows)

Line a rimmed baking sheet with wax paper and place in the freezer for at least 30 minutes. Transfer the gelato from the freezer to the refrigerator and leave to soften until fairly easy to scoop, about 20 minutes.

Using a #10 or 3-ounce ice cream scooper and working quickly, spoon out 10 scoops of gelato and place, evenly spaced, on the wax paper. Freeze for at least 4 hours or overnight.

Line a second rimmed baking sheet with wax paper and place in the freezer for at least 30 minutes while you make the ganache.

Remove the gelato balls from the freezer and spear each ball with an ice pop stick or chopstick. Dip the gelato balls into the ganache and turn to coat (the longer you submerge the gelato and the colder the ganache, the thicker the coating). Remove from the ganache and hold above the

(recipe continues)

bowl for a few seconds to catch any drippings. Place each truffle on the baking sheet and return to the freezer (you can either keep the stick in or remove it). Freeze until firm, about 2 hours, before serving. If you're making the truffles ahead of time, wrap them in wax paper and twist around the wooden stick to seal; they will keep for up to 2 days.

CHOCOLATE GANACHE

Any leftover ganache will keep in the refrigerator for up to a week; gently rewarm it, adding a little cream if needed to make it pourable, and drizzle on gelato or try dipping strawberries or other berries in it.

8 ounces chocolate (bittersweet, semisweet, or white chocolate), finely chopped

¾ cup heavy cream

2 tablespoons unsalted butter

Place the chocolate in a small, deep heat-proof bowl.

In a medium saucepan, combine the cream and butter. Place over medium-low heat and cook just until tiny bubbles form around the edges, whisking to incorporate the butter into the cream. Pour the mixture over the chocolate and set aside for 5 minutes. Gently whisk until the chocolate is completely melted and the ganache is smooth and thick. Let cool a little (the optimal temperature is 90 to 110°F). If the ganache cools too much and becomes too thick, set the bowl in a large pan of hot water and stir until it thins.

Gelato & Sorbetto Cakes—These cakes are truly memorable and are deceptively simple to make; the only requirement is that you make them a day ahead so you can soften the individual flavors and freeze them in the cake mold. You'll need a 9-inch round silicone mold that is at least 3 inches deep (see Sources, page 174) for these recipes, though you could make an all-gelato or all-sorbetto dessert with a mold of any shape and size; it's as easy as filling the mold with gelato and freezing.

We recommend a silicone mold because it's easy to use. If you don't have a silicone mold, use a springform pan or a baking pan lined with plastic wrap for easy removal.

The mold will hold 3 quarts of gelato or sorbetto without the génoise cake or 2 quarts with the génoise.

SORBETTO CAKE

This "cake" is absolutely gorgeous, and the contrasting flavors offer a real taste sensation. You also could use any of your favorite flavor combinations or a single flavor. Skip the chocolate ganache to delight your vegan friends with this dessert.

SERVES 10 TO 12

1 quart Raspberry Sorbetto (page 123)

1 quart Coconut Sorbetto (page 137)

1 quart Fresh Mango Sorbetto (page 119)

Chocolate Ganache (page 161), optional

Place the Raspberry Sorbetto in the refrigerator for 30 minutes to soften to a spreadable consistency, or make a fresh batch and pour it straight from the ice cream machine. Place a 9 by 3-inch round silicone mold on a baking dish and spread the sorbetto evenly over the mold. Freeze for 2 hours, or until the sorbetto is solid enough that it won't bleed with the second flavor.

Place the Coconut Sorbetto in the refrigerator for 30 minutes to soften or make a fresh batch. Spread the sorbetto evenly over the first layer. Freeze for 2 hours, or until solid enough that it won't bleed with the final flavor.

Place the Mango Sorbetto in the refrigerator for 30 minutes to soften or make a fresh batch. Spread the sorbetto evenly over the second layer. Freeze for 2 hours, then cover with plastic wrap and freeze solid, at least 4 hours or overnight.

To unmold the cake, place a serving platter over the top of the mold, invert the cake, and gently push the mold away from the cake until it is released. (If you're using a baking pan lined with plastic wrap for your cake, let the cake stand at room temperature for 10 minutes. Lift by the plastic overhang to loosen the cake from the pan and invert the cake onto a serving plate; pull off the plastic.)

If using the ganache, pour it over the cake and, using a metal spatula, push it quickly and gently over the edges so it coats the sides. Serve immediately, or return to the freezer and freeze for about 1 hour, until the ganache is solid. Then cover with plastic and freeze until ready to serve.

An Elegant Scoop

For a beautiful presentation, try scooping your gelato into oval shapes called quenelles. First, soften the gelato slightly and have ready a bowl of hot water and two large dessert spoons. Dip one of the spoons in the hot water, scoop out the gelato, then use the second spoon to form it into an oval shape, transferring the gelato back and forth between the two spoons until the scoop is evenly shaped and perfectly smooth.

GELATO CAKE

We make our gelato cake with génoise, a light sponge like cake that takes its name from the city of Genoa. In French pastries it is often soaked in a sweet syrup or liqueur before it is frosted. This recipe is for the classic chocolate-vanilla combination, but any flavors—such as Bacio Gelato (page 42) and Hazelnut Gelato (page 39) or Coffee Gelato (page 50) and a single-origin chocolate (see pages 28 and 30)—would be great choices.

SERVES 10 TO 12

Génoise Cake (recipe follows)

1 quart vanilla gelato (pages 26–27)

Simple Syrup (page 118)

1 quart chocolate gelato (page 28)

Chocolate Ganache (page 161)

To prepare the génoise for your gelato cake, place the génoise on a lazy Susan. Using a serrated knife, cut along the cake's equator, turning and keeping the knife level with the lazy Susan at all times to cut straight through and make 2 even layers.

Place the vanilla gelato in the refrigerator for 30 minutes to soften to a spreadable consistency, or make a fresh batch and pour it straight from the ice cream machine. Place a 9-inch round silicone mold on a baking dish and spread the gelato evenly over the mold. Brush the cut side of one of the génoise layers generously with simple syrup and place on top of the gelato, cut side down. Gently press so the cake sticks to the gelato. Cover with plastic wrap and freeze for at least 2 hours.

Place the chocolate gelato in the refrigerator for 30 minutes to soften or make a fresh batch. Spread the gelato evenly over the first génoise layer. Generously brush the cut side of the second layer of génoise with simple syrup and place cut side down over the gelato; gently press so the cake sticks to the gelato. Cover with plastic wrap and freeze until frozen solid, at least 4 hours or overnight.

To unmold the cake, place a serving platter over the top of the mold, invert the cake, and gently push the mold away from the cake until it is released. (If you're using a baking

(recipe continues)

pan lined with plastic wrap for your cake, let the cake stand at room temperature for 10 minutes. Lift by the plastic overhang to loosen the cake from the pan and invert the cake onto a serving plate; pull off the plastic wrap.)

Pour the ganache over the cake and, using a metal spatula, push it quickly and gently over the edges so it coats the sides of the cake. Smooth the top and sides. Serve immediately, or return the cake to the freezer and freeze for about 1 hour until the ganache is solid. Then cover with plastic wrap and freeze until ready to serve.

GÉNOISE CAKE

MAKES ONE 9-INCH ROUND CAKE

2 tablespoons unsalted butter, plus more for the pan

1 cup cake flour, sifted, plus more for the pan

4 large eggs, at room temperature

⅔ cup sugar

1 teaspoon pure vanilla extract

⅛ teaspoon salt

Preheat the oven to 350°F. Butter a 9-inch round cake pan and line with parchment paper. Butter and flour the parchment, knocking out any excess flour.

In a small saucepan, melt the 2 tablespoons of butter over low heat and set aside.

In the bowl of a stand mixer, combine the eggs, sugar, vanilla, and salt. Beat the mixture on high speed, scraping the sides occasionally, until it has tripled in volume and is thick enough to form a ribbon that takes a couple of seconds to dissolve when the beater is lifted, 5 to 7 minutes.

Using a rubber spatula, gently fold the 1 cup flour into the batter a third at a time until just incorporated, taking care not to remove air from the batter. Gently fold in the melted butter.

Pour the batter into the prepared pan and smooth the top evenly with a rubber spatula. Bake for 20 to 30 minutes, until the top is lightly golden, the cake springs back when gently pressed, and a wooden skewer inserted in the center comes out clean. Do not open the oven for the first 20 minutes or the cake may fall.

Transfer the cake to a wire rack to cool for 20 minutes, then run a butter knife between the cake and the side of the pan. Invert the pan onto a platter, remove the pan from the cake, and peel off the parchment. Invert the cake again onto the wire rack and let cool completely.

Gelato Sandwiches (the Ottimo)—Although the

ice cream sandwich is a traditional American favorite, finding a really good one isn't always so easy. That's why Ciao Bella came up with the Ottimo. Italian for "the best," the Ottimo is a handcrafted gelato cookie sandwich made with freshly baked cookies from Eleni's of New York, a wonderful bakery.

Eleni Gianopulos has generously shared her recipes for Lemon Cookies (page 170) and Oatmeal Raisin Cookies (page 80), and we at Ciao Bella have provided a few ideas to get you started. But just about anything goes when you're making an Ottimo; you can use any of your favorite cookies, either homemade or store-bought.

How to Assemble a Gelato Sandwich

Place a cookie, flat side up, on a work surface. Place a round scoop of slightly softened gelato on the center of the cookie, leaving plenty of room around the gelato, then place a second cookie over the gelato, flat side down. Press down until the gelato reaches the edge of the cookie, then smooth the sides using a small spoon or offset spatula. Repeat with the remaining cookies and gelato. Tightly wrap each sandwich with plastic wrap and freeze until the gelato is firm, at least 1 hour. Place the sandwiches in the refrigerator for about 30 minutes before eating to soften a little. They will keep frozen for up to 1 week.

A Few Gelato Sandwich Combinations

Chocolate cookies with vanilla gelato (pages 26–27) or chocolate gelato (page 28)—the classic sandwich

Lemon Cookies (page 170) with Lemon Gelato (page 96)—one of Ciao Bella's most popular Ottimo flavors

Oatmeal Raisin Cookies (page 80) with Cinnamon Gelato (page 56)—a take on Ciao Bella's Cinnamon with Oatmeal Cookie Gelato (page 80)

Chocolate chip cookies with chocolate gelato (page 28) or Espresso Gelato (page 52)

Ginger cookies with Maple Walnut Gelato (page 74)

Molasses cookies with Mexican Coffee Gelato (page 103)

ELENI'S LEMON COOKIES

These lightly flavored, delicate cookies are absolutely divine. The Lemon Ottimo is made with Lemon Gelato (page 96), but lemon cookies go well with many other flavors: try Strawberry Gelato (page 64), any type of vanilla gelato (see pages 26–27), Crème Fraîche Gelato (page 90), Rose Petal Gelato (page 97), or any of your favorites. You can also visit Eleni's bakery in New York and buy her cookies there or order them online (see Sources, page 174).

MAKES ABOUT 3 DOZEN

3 cups all-purpose flour

2 teaspoons cream of tartar

1 teaspoon baking soda

¼ teaspoon salt

1 cup (2 sticks) unsalted butter, at room temperature

1⅔ cups sugar

3 large eggs, at room temperature

2 tablespoons lemon extract

Preheat the oven to 350°F. Line 2 baking sheets with parchment paper and set aside.

In a medium bowl, sift together the flour, cream of tartar, baking soda, and salt.

In the bowl of a stand mixer fitted with the paddle attachment, cream the butter with the sugar until light and fluffy, about 2 minutes. Add the eggs one at a time, beating well after each addition and scraping down the sides of the bowl as needed. Add the lemon extract and mix until smooth. Stir in the flour mixture.

Scoop the batter by tablespoonfuls and roll into balls; place the balls 2 inches apart on the lined baking sheets. Bake for 15 minutes, or until very lightly golden and just firm to the touch. Remove from the oven and let cool completely. Cool the baking sheets and continue to make cookies with the remaining dough.

“WE MAKE CIAO BELLA gelato a frozen dessert that New Yorkers can be proud of, and that means a commitment to the best ingredients and a hands-on manufacturing process, core values that Eleni's also shares.**”**

—CHARLIE APT, PRESIDENT, CIAO BELLA

FESTA LIMONATA

This drink is extra-special if you use home-made lemonade. The recipe makes enough for two servings of lemonade; invite a friend over to join you, or save the remaining lemonade for another day.

Simple Syrup made with ½ cup sugar (page 118)

2 cups water

½ cup fresh lemon juice

One 4-ounce scoop Blood Orange Sorbetto (page 120) or Raspberry Sorbetto (page 123)

1 fresh mint sprig

To make the lemonade, in a pitcher, whisk together the simple syrup, water, and lemon juice. Refrigerate until ready to serve.

Pour half of the lemonade into a tall glass. Add the sorbetto, garnish with the mint sprig, and serve.

GREEN TEA SERENO

We use delicately sweet and flowery sencha tea in our Green Tea Sereno. *Sencha* means "roasted tea," and it is different from other types of green tea in that the leaves are pan-roasted or steamed and rolled rather than left flat or ground. It has slightly less caffeine than other green teas, and its clean, light flavor lends itself well to iced drinks.

SERVES 1

1½ cups chilled sencha green tea

One 4-ounce scoop Lemon Sorbetto (page 124)

1 lemon slice

Pour the tea into a tall glass. Add the sorbetto, garnish with the lemon slice, and serve.

MELON SOUP WITH MINT SYRUP

Fruit soups are a nice change of pace, are beautiful to look at, and offer a smooth ending to a summer dinner. The mint syrup adds a sweet but cooling finish.

SERVES 4

MINT SYRUP

¼ cup water

3 tablespoons sauvignon blanc wine

¼ cup granulated sugar

10 large mint leaves

2 tablespoons confectioners' sugar

1 teaspoon fresh lemon juice

1 teaspoon crème de menthe liqueur (optional)

MELON SOUP

1 cantaloupe, cut in half, seeds removed, peeled and cut into chunks

1 cup fresh orange juice

2 tablespoons fresh lime juice

2 tablespoons sugar

4 small scoops Lemon Sorbetto (page 124)

To make the mint syrup, in a medium saucepan, combine the water, wine, and granulated sugar. Place over medium heat and bring to a simmer, whisking to dissolve the sugar. Reduce the heat and simmer, whisking, for 4 minutes.

Place the mint leaves and confectioners' sugar in a food processor and puree (blending with sugar prevents the leaves from discoloring).

Whisk the mint puree, lemon juice, and crème de menthe, if using, into the wine syrup until the sugar is dissolved. Transfer to a bowl and let cool completely. Cover and refrigerate until ready to serve.

To make the soup, in a blender, combine the cantaloupe, orange juice, lime juice, and sugar and blend until smooth and the sugar is dissolved.

Ladle into 4 dessert bowls and add a scoop of sorbetto to each. Stir the mint syrup, spoon a little bit over each bowl, and serve immediately.

SOURCES

BELGIAN SHOP
www.belgianshop.com
Belgian beers

BUONITALIA IMPORTED ITALIAN FOOD
www.buonitalia.com
75 Ninth Avenue
New York, NY 10011
212-633-9090
Bronte pistachios

CHEFS CATALOG
www.chefscatalog.com
800-338-3232
Ice cream machines and thermometers

CHOCOSPHERE
www.chocosphere.com
877-992-4626
Single-origin chocolates and gianduja

COLD MOLDS
www.coldmolds.com
800-906-7221
Silicone cake molds

DITALIA
www.ditalia.com
888-260-2192
Amaretti di Saronno cookies

ELENI'S NEW YORK
www.elenis.com
75 Ninth Avenue
New York, NY 10011
888-435-3647
Brownies and cookies

KALUSTYAN'S
www.kalustyans.com
123 Lexington Avenue
New York, NY 10016
800-352-3451
Spices, Bronte pistachios, bulk chocolate, candied rose petal pieces, rosewater, dried chile powder, and vanilla beans and extract

KING ARTHUR FLOUR
www.kingarthurflour.com
800-827-6836
Bulk chocolate for gelato base and malt powder

MEXGROCER.COM
www.mexgrocer.com
877-463-9476
Cajeta, dulce de leche, and Mexican vanilla

SUR LA TABLE
www.surlatable.com
800-243-0852
Retail stores in many cities
Ice cream machines and thermometers

SWEETRIOT CHOCOLATES
www.sweetriot.com
Chocolate-covered cacao nibs and unBars

SYMPATHY FOR THE KETTLE
www.sympathyforthekettle.com
Various teas (matcha and sencha can also be found in Japanese groceries) and dried lemon verbena

WHOLE FOODS MARKET
www.wholefoodsmarkets.com
Stores throughout the country
Belgian beers, bulk chocolate, sweetriot chocolates, and various teas

WILLIAMS-SONOMA
www.williams-sonoma.com
Retail stores in many cities
877-812-6235
Ice cream machines and thermometers

INDEX

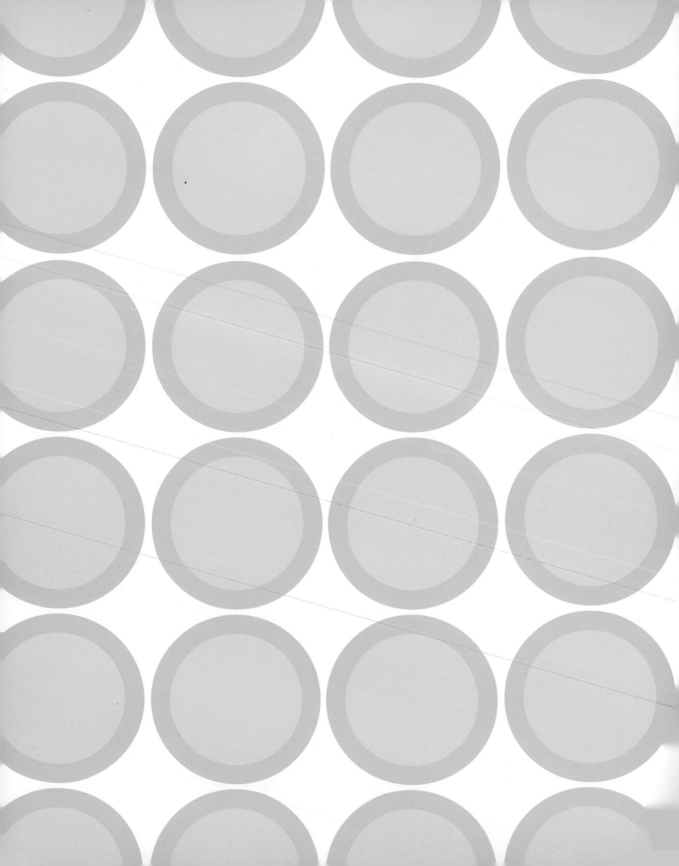